Hemingway's HEROES

Hemingway's

H E R O E S

By

Delbert E. Wylder

UNIVERSITY OF

NEW MEXICO PRESS

Excerpts from the following works by Ernest Hemingway are used by permission of Charles Scribner's Sons:
Across the River and into the Trees (Copyright 1950 Ernest Hemingway); *A Farewell to Arms* (Copyright 1929 Charles Scribner's Sons; renewal copyright © 1957 Ernest Hemingway); *For Whom the Bell Tolls* (Copyright 1940 Ernest Hemingway; renewal copyright © 1968 Mary Hemingway); *The Old Man and the Sea* (Copyright 1952 Ernest Hemingway); *The Sun Also Rises* (Copyright 1926 Charles Scribner's Sons; renewal copyright 1954 Ernest Hemingway); *To Have and Have Not* (Copyright 1937 Ernest Hemingway; renewal copyright © 1965 Mary Hemingway); and *The Torrents of Spring* (Copyright 1926 Charles Scribner's Sons; renewal copyright 1954 Ernest Hemingway).

Quotations from the following works are used by permission of Charles Scribner's Sons: Carlos Baker (ed.). *Ernest Hemingway: Critiques of Four Major Novels.* (New York: Charles Scribner's Sons, 1962.); Andrew Turnbull (ed.). *The Letters of F. Scott Fitzgerald.* (New York: Charles Scribner's Sons, 1963.); William Ralph Inge. *Christian Mysticism.* (New York: Charles Scribner's Sons, 1899.); Maxwell Perkins, *Editor to Author: The Letters of Maxwell E. Perkins* (with an Introduction by John Hall Wheelock, ed.). (New York: Charles Scribner's Sons, 1950.); and S. L. Frank (ed.). *A Soloviev Anthology* (translated by Natalie Dunnington). (New York: Charles Scribner's Sons, 1950.)

Chapter I, on *The Torrents of Spring,* is a revised version of an article which appeared in *The South Dakota Review,* Winter. 1967-68, and is being used through the courtesy of *The South Dakota Review* and its editor, John R. Milton.

for
Edith

Acknowledgments

ALL WRITERS OF applied criticism owe first acknowledgment to the author of the original material from which the critical work has grown. I have been especially fortunate in subject matter, for Hemingway was one of those writers who bear re-reading. He hoped that he could write truly enough so that his work would be valid in a year, or ten years, or always, and the continued publication of Hemingway criticism is a testament to his success.

The published criticism is the second area of my indebtedness. It is difficult to determine just how much one's thinking has depended on the ideas of others. Hemingway has had some fine critics, and I owe much to those with whom I have both agreed and disagreed Most of these critics' names will be found in the bibliography, but I would especially like to thank Carlos Baker, the late Charles Fenton, Sheridan Baker, Earl Rovit, Philip Young, and Robert W Lewis, Jr., for their exceptional works.

Hemingway once acknowledged his writing debt to Gertrude Stein and Ezra Pound. Of Pound, he said, "Ezra was always right." I was fortunate to have such a critic. It would be impossible to overstate my debt to Professor John C. Gerber. His detailed comments and suggestions, as well as his encouragement, are responsible for much that may be called good in this work. I owe a tremendous debt of gratitude for his patience and wisdom. I also owe special thanks to Professors Sherman Paul, Alexander Kern, and Charles T. Miller of the University of Iowa and to Professor Max Westbrook of the University of Texas.

I would also like to thank the many friends, students, and family members who have over a period of years sent me Hemingway materials and have listened to and criticized my ideas on Hemingway, especially colleagues like Professors George Arms, Donald Greene, and J. Golden Taylor. I have learned from them all, and especially in the classes of Professors Gerber, Kern, Miller, Paul Engle, Hansford Martin, Ray B. West, Bernard Baum, and the late Bartholow V. Crawford at the University of Iowa.

Quotations from the following works are used by permission of the publishers: (1) E. P. Dutton & Co., Inc.: George Snell. *The Shapers of American Fiction*. (New York: E. P. Dutton & Co., 1947.); and Van Wyck Brooks. *On Literature Today*. (New York: E. P. Dutton & Co., Inc., 1941.) (2) Houghton Mifflin Company: Henry Seidel Canby. *American Memoir*. (Boston: Houghton Mifflin Co., 1947.); and Arthur Mizener. *The Far Side of Paradise: A Biography of F. Scott Fitzgerald*. (Boston: Houghton Mifflin Co., 1951.) (3) Random House, Inc.: A. E. Hotchner. *Papa Hemingway*. (New York: Random House, Inc., 1966.); and Lord Raglan. *The Hero: A Study in Tradition, Myth, and Drama*. (New York: Random House, Inc., 1956.) (4) Twayne Publishers, Inc.: Earl Rovit. *Ernest Hemingway*. (New York: Twayne Publishers, Inc., 1963.) (5) University of Kentucky Press: John Killinger. *Hemingway and the Dead Gods: A Study in Existentialism*. (Lexington, Ky.: University of Kentucky Press, 1960.) (6) Princeton University Press: Carlos Baker. *Hemingway: the Writer as Artist*. (Princeton, N.J.: Princeton University Press, 1956). (7) Southern Methodist University Press: W. M. Frohock. *The Novel of Violence in America, 1920-1950*. (Dallas: Southern Methodist University Press, 1950.)

Quotations from the following work are used by permission of the author: Robert W. Lewis, *Hemingway on Love*. (Austin, Texas: University of Texas Press, 1965.)

Finally, my thanks to Edith Wylder, who contributed so much

to this work. Who typed it in a succession of drafts, who proofread it, edited it, criticized it. Whose suggestions were valuable and whose inspiration was invaluable. Who saw to it that I had the time for writing, and from whom I learned much.

Contents

Hemingway's HEROES

INTRODUCTION

"Mr. Hemingway, do you give
credence to the theory of a
recurring hero in all of your works?
Answer: Does Yogi Berra
have a grooved swing?"[1]
　　　　　　　　　—Ernest Hemingway

SO MUCH HAS BEEN WRITTEN on the Hemingway "hero" that it might seem unproductive to undertake another examination of this literary phenomenon. But I believe that one of the longstanding problems of Hemingway criticism has been the failure to disentangle the Hemingway personality, as evidenced in his life and in his nonfictional statements, from the characters that he has created for his novels. Coupled with this tendency to link Hemingway with his protagonists, despite his own often vehement objections, has been an equal proclivity to view the Hemingway protagonist as a recurring hero in a progression of novels so that the critical treatment of the Hemingway hero has become almost an exercise in fictional biography. Nick Adams grows into Jake Barnes into Frederic Henry into Robert Jordan into Richard Cantwell; all are considered to be one character at different ages. The

result, unfortunately, has been that the recurring biographical hero has provided almost the sole critical focus for the
interpretation of separate novels which are unique artistic
creations, distinctive not only in the concept of the hero
and his environments but in artistic techniques as well.
That critical focus, it seems to me, has frequently forced
a preconceived and rigid pattern upon the interpretation
of some of Hemingway's novels. This is particularly unfortunate, for such a view does not allow a demonstration
of Hemingway's artistic versatility, his experimentation,
and his increasing skill as a writer.

This study of the Hemingway hero will focus on the
hero as he appears in the individual novels, and will consider each novel as a separate entity with its own distinctive
artistic unity and its own distinctive protagonist. Of major
importance in this consideration of the novels will be an
analysis of the narrative perspective from which Hemingway tells the story. The examination of the separate novels
reveals a different emphasis, a picture of Hemingway gradually changing his artistic concepts as he sees the role of the
hero changing as the world becomes more complex. Most
of all, what becomes apparent is an Ernest Hemingway
who continues to mature as an artist.

Linking Hemingway with his fictional heroes has been
part of Hemingway criticism for many years. Despite his
objection to biographical criticism, Hemingway frequently
gave impetus to the critical practice by remarks during
personal interviews in which he often portrayed himself
as a "Nick Adams" type of boy. As a matter of fact, he
succeeded in creating a legend surrounding "Papa" Hem-

ingway that has hidden many of the facts of his life. Further, he has, like many other authors, often used rather thinly disguised autobiographical materials as the basis for his writing. Much of the early criticism reflects the attitude expressed by Granville Hicks in 1935—that from Hemingway's first novels and short stories "there emerges a sort of composite character, the Hemingway hero, whose story is, in its broad outlines, the story not merely of Hemingway's life but of the lives of a not inconsiderable group of his contemporaries."[2] But Hicks made an important distinction in his analysis, a distinction that in one form or another still exists in the criticism of the Hemingway hero. He suggested that there was not just one Hemingway hero, "but two heroes: the autobiographical hero . . . and the hero that Hemingway is not but thinks he would like to be."[3]

This distinction was neglected for a time, and critics continued to concentrate on the biographical nature of Hemingway's heroes. In 1947, George Snell could say that "All the principal Hemingway heroes . . . are one and the same person, and they are largely modeled upon Hemingway himself."[4] In 1952, however, a book appeared that included one of the most detailed examinations of the Hemingway hero, Philip Young's *Ernest Hemingway*. In this work Young examines the traumatic effects of experience on the individual which result in a "wounded" hero. Like Granville Hicks, Young makes a sharp distinction between this sensitive wounded hero and another type of hero, who, through his acceptance of a code, finds the strength to face the vicissitudes of life. Young traces the wounded hero,

Nick Adams, through the short stories, links him with the heroes of the novels, and then equates the "wounded hero" with Hemingway.

The hero is a twentieth-century American, born, raised and hurt in the Middle West, who like all of us, has been going through life with the marks his experiences have made on him. The outlaws and professional sportsmen who have appeared along the way have taught the man to try to live by a code, but they are not the man himself. What is more, the lessons have not always been of the sort the hero can immediately master.[5]

Those who give the "hero" a code to live by are what Young calls the "code-heroes." They are the ones who *can* and *do* live by the code. Their lives are so conditioned by and to the code that nothing in experience, whether physical pain or psychological motivation or confrontation with death, will cause them to be unfaithful to their code of honor, or what Hemingway in *Death in the Afternoon* called *pundonor,* a more inclusive word which means "honor, probity, courage, self-respect and pride in one word."[6]

Perhaps Carlos Baker's *Ernest Hemingway: The Writer as Artist* (1956),[7] although a critical biography, least obviously ties the Hemingway hero to the Hemingway personality. For the most part, Baker separates the biographical sections of his work from the critical sections and analyzes the major novels, in particular, from such a variety of critical approaches that the Hemingway personality, though sometimes intrusive, is seldom confused with the protagonists of the novels.

Works such as John Killinger's *Hemingway and the Dead Gods: A Study in Existentialism* (1965),[8] which have attempted to identify Hemingway's philosophical position, have generally projected an image of Hemingway writing out his life story, and thus have followed those evaluations which present Hemingway as his own hero. Killinger, however, does distinguish between the Hemingway protagonists. There are the heroes who operate by the code and the *cobardes*, or cowards, who for one reason or another cannot operate by it.

A recent important full-length critical work on Hemingway, Earl Rovit's *Ernest Hemingway*,[9] continues with another adaptation of the Granville Hicks-Philip Young separation of hero types. Rovit refers to the Nick Adams hero as the *tyro* and to the "code-hero" as the *tutor*; for, he says,

it is basically an educational relationship, albeit a very one-sided one, which binds them together. The tyro, faced with the overwhelming confusion and hurt (nada) inherent in an attempt to live an active sensual life, admires the deliberate self-containment of the tutor (a much "simpler man") who is seemingly not beset with inner uncertainties. Accordingly, the tyro tries to model his behavior on the pattern he discerns. However, the tyro is not a simple man; being in fact a very near projection of Hemingway himself, he is never able to attain the state of serene unself-consciousness—what James once called nastily "the deep intellectual repose"—that seems to come naturally to the tutor.[10]

Rovit has not only recapitulated the nature of the two types of the Hemingway hero as identified by Young, but has continued with the identification of one of the types, the tyro, with the writer himself. The tutor figure, on the other hand, preserves the characteristic of the type of person Hemingway would "like to be" that Granville Hicks suggested in 1935. An even more recent study of Hemingway's major works, Robert W. Lewis' *Hemingway on Love*,[11] has broken new ground in Hemingway criticism, breaking essentially from previous patterns of the hero. Lewis discusses Hemingway by contrasting elements of *eros* and *agape* in the thematic development of various works. Although he sometimes makes use of the progressive hero concept and sometimes reads the short stories as autobiographical in part, he is always aware of the dangers. Generally his emphasis is on the separate works of art, and he is never overly dependent on preconceived theories.

What has developed over a period of decades is a theory which associates Hemingway's life and personality quite closely with at least one type of Hemingway hero, and his hopes and ideals with the other type. The criticism that has resulted has been, without a doubt, both interesting and enlightening. Rovit's analysis of *The Sun Also Rises,* for example, is one of the best discussions of the novel on record. But there have also been disadvantages to this direction in Hemingway criticism. The attempt to see the Hemingway protagonist as a projection of Hemingway recurring over and over again in successive novels has been restrictive in forcing most of the criticism into a biographical pattern. The criticisms become dependent on the corpus of Hemingway writing rather than on an attempt to see each novel in terms of its own artistic unity. Moreover, such an overall view has frequently resulted in a distortion of the novel under consideration at the time.

There is the need for further study of the Hemingway hero, but not along the lines that have already been explored. Rather, there needs to be a reexamination with a concentration on the separate consideration of each novel and with the emphasis on the differences rather than the similarities among the protagonists of each work. What emerges, I believe, is a different picture of the Hemingway protagonist.[12]

I

THE
TORRENTS
OF SPRING:

A Parody of the sentimental HERO

PRACTICALLY NO CRITICAL interest has been shown
Ernest Hemingway's first published novel, *The Torrents
of Spring*. There are a number of reasons for this oversight,
all of which may be more or less valid, but it has been unfortunate that critics have neglected to relate this work to
the rest of Hemingway's literary canon. One of the reasons
that the first novel has not been examined closely in the
predominant, biographically oriented criticism has been
that it does not provide an example of the Hemingway
hero as either the wounded hero or the code hero. There
are other reasons. The work was written hurriedly[1]; it
may have been written with the practical motive of breaking a contract[2]; it was printed in a small edition[3]; and it
is unlike the rest of Hemingway's novels in that it is a direct

satire. Since it is primarily a satire on two novels by Sherwood Anderson, it provides a number of important insights into the Hemingway hero by highlighting what Hemingway obviously thought were ridiculous aspects of the Andersonian hero.

Carlos Baker makes an appropriate comparison when he suggests that in relation to Anderson's *Dark Laughter* the travesty "stood about as Fielding's *Shamela* did to Richardson's *Pamela.*"[4] Possibly Hemingway had the *Pamela-Shamela* relationship in mind, since he prefaces his work and introduces each of the four parts with quotations from Fielding. The comparison to *Shamela* is only suggestive since Hemingway expands his satire into a rather inclusive attack on other writers as well.[5] But it is true that the most important and the most consistent attack is on Sherwood Anderson, his narrative technique, and the heroes of his last two novels.

As F. Scott Fitzgerald reported to Maxwell Perkins, "I agree with Ernest that Anderson's last two books have let everybody down who believed in him. . . ."[6] The "last two books" were *Many Marriages* and *Dark Laughter,* both of which are centered around a hero who has stopped at middle age to reexamine his life in relation to his environment. In each case the protagonist sees his life and his capitalistic, "Puritan," middlewestern, American society as sterile and without meaning. The impotence of his sexual life serves, in both cases, as a central image for the meaninglessness that has resulted from the repressions and restrictions of the life around him.

John Webster, in *Many Marriages,* begins to question his life, suddenly confronts one of his young female employees, and gradually becomes enamoured of her. He takes her for a stroll into the country, makes love to her, and then makes plans to leave his wife. He prepares a small shrine in his own room, complete with candles, a picture of the Virgin, and a mirror, and walks naked in front of the mirror. Finally, still naked, he confronts his wife and daughter and explains to them the fundamental beauty of sex. Afterwards he leaves with the young woman, Natalie, not knowing that his wife will commit suicide.

In *Dark Laughter,* John Stockton leaves his reporting job and his wife to return to a small town where he had lived as a boy. He takes a job in a wheel factory, changes his name to Bruce Dudley, makes friends with a worker named Sponge Martin, and finally leaves his factory job when he is hired by the factory-owner's wife, Aline Grey, as a gardener. While Aline's husband is marching in a parade of World War I veterans, Aline wanders into the garden and Bruce Dudley recognizes that the right moment has arrived. He challenges her with his eyes, and follows her into the house and up to her bedroom. He disappears immediately afterwards. Several months later he returns to the now pregnant Aline, confronts her husband, and takes her away with him. The novel ends with the husband, who had momentarily considered suicide, sitting rigidly in bed listening to the primitive laughter of Negro maidservants below. Bruce Dudley, however, has already started to wonder whether he has found the right woman, even as John Webster wonders about his choice toward the conclusion of *Many Marriages*. As the narrator of *Dark Laughter* explains,

> Odd that he, wanting her so much and now that he had got her, began almost at once thinking of something else. He had wanted to find the right woman, a woman he could really marry, but that was only half of it. He wanted to find the right kind of work too.[7]

The plot summaries, of course, do not indicate the technical complexity of the novels, nor the specific characteristics of the protagonists. In both novels the protagonists are pictured as so emotional, so self-conscious, and so wounded that it is little wonder Hemingway found them ripe subjects for ridicule.

It should be remembered that *The Torrents of Spring* was written *after* Hemingway had completed the first draft of *The Sun Also Rises*.[8] He had already created in detail two characters who in some respects resembled the Anderson protagonists.[9] Robert Cohn is the psychologically wounded man, self-conscious and emotional to the point of sentimentality. Like the Anderson heroes, he believes that a change of scenery and a change in his love-life will solve the problems of his own inadequacy. Jake Barnes, too, is wounded, self-conscious, and frequently emotional, but he does not act like Robert Cohn or the Anderson heroes. Jake does not believe in any sudden miraculous cures.

Another important difference between Anderson's heroes and Jake Barnes is that Jake Barnes has been wounded both physically and psychologically in the war.

The Anderson protagonists show only the psychological
scars of their experiences. Frequently we are unaware
what it is that has so badly damaged an Anderson hero.
For example, Bruce Dudley is impotent until almost the
end of *Dark Laughter*. In his reflections on childhood and
his married life, Bruce reveals a psychological attachment
to his mother and a highly competitive and unsatisfactory
relationship with his wife. Neither of these complications,
however, is developed sufficiently as explanations of impotency. In *The Torrents of Spring,* Yogi Johnson, Hemingway's counterpart for Bruce Dudley, is also impotent.
Hemingway does not expose the reason for his impotency
until late in the novel when he tells the story of how, in
Paris after the war, Yogi had been seduced by a beautiful
lady. A "beautiful thing" (Anderson's expression for sexual
intercourse) had happened to him, but he discovers later
at a Parisian peep-show that the "beautiful thing" had been
witnessed by a large paying audience.

In both Anderson novels and in Hemingway's parody,
the cure for impotency is a quiet, willing woman. Neither
Aline Grey in *Dark Laughter* nor Natalie in *Many Marriages* says a word in the scenes which lead to their seduc-
tion. In *The Torrents of Spring* Yogi's impotence is cured
when a squaw wearing only moccasins walks into Brown's
Beanery. This event causes a certain amount of confusion
for most of the customers, but Yogi reacts quite differently.

*Something had broken inside of him. Something had snapped
as the squaw came into the room. He had a new feeling. A
feeling he thought had been lost for ever. Lost for always.
Lost. Gone permanently.*[10]

Yogi has regained his masculinity through seeing the primitive naked squaw. Such an exaggeration of the original psychological wound and the ease with which the cure is effected successfully satirizes the psychologically wounded and easily cured Anderson hero.

Other passages in *The Torrents of Spring* also reflect Hemingway's apparent attitude toward Anderson's excessive concentration on the wounded man. Yogi Johnson reveals to two Indian companions that he had been in the war.

"White chief shoot pool?" the big Indian asked.

"No," Yogi Johnson said. "My right arm was crippled in the war."

"White chief have hard luck," the small Indian said. "Shoot one game of Kelly pool."

"He got both arms and both legs shot off at Ypres," the big Indian said in an aside to Yogi. "Him very sensitive."

"All right," Yogi said. "I'll shoot one game."[11]

The protagonist, who has been attempting to gain sympathy for his war wounds, is humiliated by the obvious severity of the Indian's wounds. When Yogi loses four dollars and thirty cents in the pool game, his humiliation is complete.

The reflective quality of the Anderson hero is another target of Hemingway's ridicule. Jake Barnes, who narrates his own story in *The Sun Also Rises,* is reflective and frequently emotional, but his narration in general shows a rational mind trying to find answers to questions about how to live in the world. Anderson's protagonists, on the other hand, are highly emotional, their thoughts are presented frequently in free-associational patterns, and they try to deal with abstract concepts—with the meaning of life, the relationship of literature and the arts to life, and the concepts of love and human relationships. Seldom do they conclude anything, but end their series of questions by "wondering." John Webster in *Many Marriages* thinks:

Had he only taken up with her because she was a kind of instrument that would help him escape from his wife and from a life he had come to detest? Was he but using her? Had he at bottom any real feeling in regard to her, and understanding of her?
He wondered.[12]

In *Dark Laughter* Bruce's reflections about his mother and all mothers deteriorates into the ridiculous in a final question about meaninglessness.

Had [his mother] become merely a figure his fancy played with? A mother, after her death, or after you no longer live near her, is something the male fancy can play with, dream of, make a part of the movement of the grotesque dance of life. Idealize her. Why not? She is gone. She will not come near to break the thread of the dream. The dream is as true as the reality. Who knows the difference? Who knows anything?[13]

In *The Torrents of Spring* Hemingway not only concisely parodies the "wondering" quality, but also burlesques it by having Yogi or Scripps O'Neil, a character based on Anderson's Sponge Martin of *Dark Laughter*, wonder about the most obvious matters.

On the railway station was written in big letters:

P E T O S K E Y

There was a pile of deer shipped down by hunters from the Upper Peninsula of Michigan, lying piled the one on the other, dead and stiff and drifted half over with snow on the station platform. Scripps read the sign again. Could this be Petoskey?

A man inside the station, tapping something back of a wicketed window. He looked out at Scripps. Could he be a telegrapher? Something told Scripps that he was.

He stepped out of the snow-drift and approached the window. Behind the window the man worked busily away at his telegrapher's key.

"Are you a telegrapher?" asked Scripps.

"Yes, sir," said the man. "I'm a telegrapher."[14]

There are other sign-reading episodes in the novel, all of which indicate the simplicity, the stupidity, or naivete of the Anderson hero. This is especially true in Hemingway's characterization of Scripps O'Neil, a parody of the simple-man character of which Anderson was inordinately fond. This type of character is more primitive than the sensitive man and is capable of doing things with his hands, or of understanding women well enough to have a satisfactory marriage. He is, in a way, the white link with the primitive Negroes in *Dark Laughter* who sense the deep mystery of life, who evidently have an unrestricted natural sex life, and who laugh downstairs in the kitchen as the frustrated middle-class whites above go to their separate bedrooms.

This simple-man hero is frequently a subject for Hemingway's attack. In *Dark Laughter* Bruce Dudley often envies Sponge Martin and his wife. Sponge is a man who chews tobacco, and on some paydays he and his wife go fishing and drinking together.

Sponge's old woman was all right. When she and Sponge were out that way, after catfish, and they had both taken five or six good stiff drinks of "moon," she was like a kid. She made Sponge feel—Lordy!

They were lying on a pile of half-rotten old sawdust near the fire, right where the old wood-yard had been. When the old woman was a little up and acted like a kid it made Sponge feel that way too. It was a cinch the old woman was a good sport. . . .[15]

Hemingway's Scripps O'Neil has two wives, one in Mancelona and one in Petoskey. The Mancelona wife is somewhat like Sponge Martin's wife.

With his wife in Mancelona Scripps often got drunk. When he was drunk he and his wife were happy. They would go down together to the railway station and walk out along the tracks, and then sit under a pine tree on a little hill that overlooked the railway and drink. Sometimes they drank all night. Sometimes they drank for a week at a time. It did them good. It made Scripps strong.[16]

Scripps O'Neil does not, however, remain a parody of Sponge Martin, for he also takes on the characteristics of the sensitive questioning hero, like the protagonists of *Many Marriages* and *Dark Laughter*. Both of these protagonists think of themselves as potential writers, and as they interpret life they have a tendency to let their "fancies" create highly romantic symbols. In short stories as well as in the novels, Anderson's characters frequently attach significance to an object such as a bird, a horse, or even a stone. John Webster creates imaginary scenes in which a stone he has found figures prominently and holds the stone as a talisman during most of his lecture to his wife and daughter. He thinks of its meanings and its relationship to the meaning of life. Finally, he gives it to his daughter during the religious ritual, explaining that it might be the "Jewel of Life," and she uses it to hold together her almost shattered world after he leaves and her mother commits suicide.

Hemingway ridicules this tendency on the part of the Anderson protagonists to project themselves into individualized symbols by having Yogi Johnson find a frozen bird lying along the railroad tracks.[17] Hemingway shows the sentimentality of such attachments in the first scene with the bird and continues to emphasize the sentimentality by having other characters comment on it.

He picked up a dead bird that had frozen and fallen onto the railroad tracks and put it inside his shirt to warm it. The bird nestled close to his warm body and pecked at his chest gratefully.

"Poor little chap," Scripps said. "You feel the cold too."

Tears came into his eyes.[18]

Later, when Scripps confronts the telegrapher, the man is so puzzled by the bird that Scripps is unable to communicate something deep within him which he wishes to share with the telegrapher.

The telegrapher looked at him curiously.

"Say," he asked, "are you a fairy?"

"No," Scripps said. "I don't know what being a fairy means."

"Well," said the telegrapher, "what do you carry a bird around for?"

"Bird?" asked Scripps. "What bird?"

"That bird that's sticking out of your shirt." Scripps was at a loss.[19]

Scripps tries to find words to explain the emotional involvements that have led him to come to this town, but can't find them.

"My wife left me," Scripps said abruptly.

"I don't wonder if you go around with a damn bird sticking out of your shirt," the telegrapher said.[20]

After Scripps "marries" an elderly waitress by taking her for a walk in the country, where a "beautiful thing" happens to them, the bird becomes a comic reminder of the incident in another descriptive passage which stylistically parodies Anderson's adaptation of the rhythms of Gertrude Stein's prose. The bird has been damaged during the physical activities of the lovers.

The frost on the windows. The warmth inside. The cold outside. Scripps's bird, rather rumpled now, sitting on the counter and preening his feathers.[21]

Finally Scripps gives the bird to the elderly waitress when he wishes to be rid of her. He has felt "deep stirrings inside him" for a younger waitress named Mandy in the same diner. As the first waitress leaves with the bird,

Mandy interrupts one of her many "literary" stories.

"That bird she just took out," Mandy was saying.
"Oh, did she take a bird out?" Scripps asked. "Go on with
the story."[22]

The bird as symbol has become completely insignificant to
Scripps now that he is romantically involved with a different woman.

Robert W. Lewis has pointed out that in Hemingway's
early writing "he writes in reaction to romantic love without quite accepting his own rejection of it."[23] Certainly
The Torrents of Spring is a good example of Hemingway's
rejection of Anderson's faith in romantic love, where sex
becomes the elixir of life. The tendency of the Anderson
protagonist to associate every aspect of life with sex, and
then to romanticize sex to the point that it becomes almost
a religion is one of the most important aspects of Hemingway's attack upon Anderson's concept of the hero. The
dark laughter of the Negroes in the Anderson novels symbolizes primitive unfettered sexuality, and Hemingway's
use of the Indian war whoop is a constant reference to the
Anderson concept. Further, Anderson's omniscient author
often comments on the stirrings or poundings within the
character. These poundings are sexual, the result of those
forces of nature that are once more released at middle age
for the Anderson heroes and are released in Hemingway's
satire by the chinook and the spring thaw. In *Dark Laughter* the stirrings cause John Webster to erect a shrine in his
room, with candles on each side of a picture of the Virgin
that he believes resembles his sweetheart Natalie. In front

of his shrine, which also includes a mirror, he strides around the room naked. Sex has become his religion. It provides the meaning of life. In the narrator's words,

Men who have passed the age of thirty and who have intelligence understand such things. A German scientist can explain perfectly. If there is anything you do not understand in human life consult the works of Dr. Freud.[24]

Hemingway's attack upon the sentimentalized sexuality of the Anderson heroes is directed at a number of the aspects of the sexual concept. First, with a witty vulgarity, he suggests that the stirrings are not always sexual; they may be the result of other physical forces.

"We are man and wife now," she said kindly. "We have just been married. What would you like to eat for supper, Scripps, dear?"

"I don't know," Scripps said. He felt vaguely uneasy. Something was stirring within him.

"Perhaps you have eaten enough of the beans, dear Scripps," the elderly waitress, now his wife, said.[25]

Second, Hemingway plays upon Anderson's habit of having his protagonist think of his new wife as his "woman," as the narrator explains John Webster's thinking, for example: "Now he was going away with Natalie, with his own woman. . . ." Hemingway collects such references into short passages to emphasize the sentimentalized thinking.

"You are my woman," he said. Tears came into her eyes, too.

"You are my man," she said.

"Once again I say: you are my woman."

Scripps pronounced the words solemnly. Something had broken inside him again. He felt he could not keep from crying.

"Let this be our wedding ceremony," the elderly waitress said.

Scripps pressed her hand. "You are my woman," he said simply.

"You are my man and more than my man." She looked into his eyes. "You are all of America to me."[26]

Most important of all is Hemingway's attack upon Anderson's basic concept that romanticized sex will provide the answers to the meaning of life. Toward the conclusion of each of Anderson's novels, the protagonist and his new woman walk out of town together. At the conclusion of *The Torrents of Spring,* Yogi regains his virility by seeing the naked squaw walk into the beanery. The more conservative people in the dining room react by hiding their faces or ordering that she be put into the snow. A Negro cook, one of Anderson's primitives, reacts more conservatively than the rest and forcibly ejects her from the diner. Yogi, however, follows her out into the snow and down the railroad tracks leading out of town.

As they walk Yogi Johnson silently strips off his garments. One by one he strips off his garments, and casts them beside the track. In the end he is clad only in a worn pair of pump-maker shoes. Yogi Johnson, naked in the moonlight, walking North beside the squaw. The squaw striding along beside him.[27]

With an escape to nudity, which figures prominently in both Anderson novels, Yogi Johnson figures in a perfect Andersonian conclusion. But in *The Torrents of Spring,* the remaining scenes destroy the effects of the romantic gesture and increase its ludicrous aspects through the actions and words of Yogi's two Indian friends who follow the couple down the tracks. They carefully retrieve all of Yogi's clothes to sell to the Salvation Army. Finally, in their very realistic comments, they indicate their skepticism of the lasting quality of love. They note that Yogi is a snappy dresser and predict that he will be coming back. Then the weather changes, the real chinook begins to blow, and the Indians feel the same stirrings Yogi has felt. Unromantically, they hurry back to town.

> "Want to get in town before rush," the tall Indian grunts.
> "Red brothers want to be well up in line," the little Indian grunts anxiously.
> "Nobody work in factory now," the tall Indian grunted.
> "Better hurry."
> The warm wind blows. Inside the Indians strange longings were stirring. They knew what they wanted. Spring at last was coming to the frozen little Northern town. The two Indians hurried along the track.[28]

Just as characters in Anderson's novels are always coming to the conclusion that they know what they want, the Indians too know what they want after feeling the strange spring torrents of longing. But they do not romanticize their longings. They know what they want in a very basic fashion. The suggestion of a lineup in a house of prostitution strips bare all of the romantic elements that Anderson's protagonists have constructed around the idea of sex.

This is an exceptionally well conceived conclusion to the satire, and makes clear the main direction of Hemingway's attack on Anderson's sexual philosophy. The Anderson protagonists have been made to appear ridiculous for their sentimentality. They have been shown to be hypersensitive to their environment, inane and self-centered in their reflections, enamoured of the symbols their imaginations have created, and finally ridiculous in their creation of a mystical religion based on the sexual impulses.

It is also important that *The Torrents of Spring* includes an attack on Anderson's method of telling the story in *Dark Laughter* and *Many Marriages*. Although the plot of each novel is quite simple, the undercurrent of psychological or psychoanalytical analysis of motivations from the past mixed with the present is frequently difficult for the reader to follow. In almost every chapter of *Dark Laughter*, for example, the time sequence is totally distorted. Chapter Eleven begins with a statement from Sponge Martin, which is followed by lyrics from some Negro songs, and then a description of the factory at Old Harbor with Bruce Dudley and Sponge Martin putting away their brushes after a day's work. As they leave the factory, Bruce's thoughts wander to his childhood, then to a Jew he had known in Chicago, back to his mother, to Aline, to his mother again, to the importance of the Mississippi River, to Chicago, and back to his mother and the river. The reader is often unsure of the time relationship involved or whose thoughts the narrator is reporting, or whether the thoughts are really the thoughts of the character or simply the narrator's interpretation of the thoughts. *The Torrents of Spring* parodies this confusing technique.

Hemingway has his characters become confused about their own identities, and finds it necessary to intrude, with tongue in cheek, in order to explain the time sequence. Finally, he makes a direct apology to the reader. The first real confusion appears as early as page five in *The Torrents of Spring,* where Scripps is thinking.

There was nothing rococo about it, like the buildings he had seen in Paris. No, he had never been in Paris. That was not he. That was his friend Yogi Johnson.[29]

From this point, Hemingway treats his material chronologically but gradually introduces some complicating flashbacks. The story centers on Scripps. At the beginning of Chapter Ten, however, the narrator intrudes to point out a break in the chronological sequence.

Spring was coming. Spring was in the air. (Author's Note.— This is the same day on which the story starts, back on page one.)[30]

But the narrator recognizes that this is not enough in the way of an explanation, and once more he intrudes for purposes of clarification.

(In case the reader is becoming confused, we are now up to where the story opened with Yogi Johnson and Scripps O'Neil in the pump-factory itself, with the chinook wind blowing. . . . . At any rate, we will now go on with Yogi Johnson. Yogi Johnson, the reader may remember, is the chap who was in the *war. As the story opens, he is just coming out of the pump-fac-tory. (See page three.)*

It is very hard to write this way, beginning things backward, and the author hopes the reader will realize this and not grudge this little word of explanation.[31]

After this point, Yogi Johnson does become the central character, and his experiences with the Indians demand no further intrusive commentary by the author. But the notes have accomplished their purpose in pointing out quite directly the obscurity and artificiality of Anderson's method of telling the story.

The major fault that Hemingway evidently saw in Anderson's narrative technique, however, was Anderson's sentimental attachment to his characters. Anderson frequently used sentimental detail in characterizing Bruce Dudley as a boy, such as having several references to the young Bruce wearing knee pants. In satirizing this tendency, Hemingway assumes the same sentimental attitude toward Scripps O'Neil.

That was when Scripps had been a little boy. He used often to ask his father: "Father, why if we come to look at the anarchists on Sunday, why can't we ride on the shoot the chutes?" He had never been satisfied with his father's answer. He had been a little boy in knee pants then.[32]

In *Winesburg, Ohio,* with a narrator close to the adolescent George Willard, and in stories like "I Want to Know Why," and "I'm a Fool" with a youthful first-person narrator, Anderson had been extremely successful. But Anderson failed in his attempt to create a "roving narrator" who flitted in and out of the minds of a number of characters and frequently identified himself with the characters. His technique is not too different from the one that Hemingway himself will use in *Across the River and Into the Trees,* but the youthful Hemingway who had just finished the first draft of *The Sun Also Rises* seemed to find this intermingling of narrator and character far from his own naturalistic directions. His attack in *The Torrents of Spring* is well calculated to exaggerate and highlight what he considered a sentimental display.

For the most part, Hemingway's satire is mock-romantic in tone. Only once does he drop the satiric mask, and then he does it in order to make a direct attack upon Anderson and another American writer, Willa Cather. Although he places the attack in a speech by Yogi Johnson, the young World War I veteran Ernest Hemingway shows through. Yogi names both writers, and begins by describing Anderson's treatment of Fred Grey's war experiences in *Dark Laughter.* Fred had killed a man in No Man's Land one night.

Afterward, killing this man haunted Fred. It's got to be sweet and true. That was the way the soldiers thought, Anderson said. The hell it was. This Fred was supposed to have been two years in an infantry regiment at the front.[33]

In a lecture that Yogi gives to two of his Indian friends, he tells them about the war and how war is. What he tells them resembles quite closely what Frederic Henry reports in *A Farewell to Arms* and what Hemingway wrote in his introduction to *Men at War,* including the effect of the loss of the sense of immortality. Finally, the diatribe in *Torrents of Spring* ends with

> Nobody had any damn business to write about it, though, that didn't at least know about it from hearsay. Literature has too strong an effect on people's minds. Like this American writer Willa Cather, who wrote a book about the war where all the last part of it was taken from the action in the "Birth of a Nation," and ex-servicemen wrote to her from all over America to tell her how much they liked it.[34]

Worst of all, Anderson had written about war without having experienced it, and it was the sentimentally romantic stance taken by Anderson, and his use of sentimental stereotypes, that caused the outburst.

Throughout the rest of the novel, Hemingway's satirical perspective remains consistent. It is little wonder that, as Philip Young has pointed out, the novel originally received "many extravagant reviews," including Allen Tate's comment that "here was the most economically realized humor of disproportion that he had read in American prose."[35] Short as it is, *The Torrents of Spring* contains a variety of attacks on Anderson and many other writers, but especially important is the attack on the Anderson hero. What the satire makes clear is that romanticized sex is not the answer to all human problems. Since Hemingway wrote it after completing the first draft of *The Sun Also Rises, The Torrents of Spring* becomes an interesting and important novel for study, especially as it emphasizes Hemingway's attitudes toward Anderson's wounded heroes.

II

THE SUN
ALSO RISES:

The Wounded Anti-HERO

HEMINGWAY CHOSE TO present *The Sun Also Rises* from the first-person narrative perspective, to have Jake Barnes tell his own story of his experiences in post-World War I France and Spain. The result is a very successful novel, and at least part of the success is attributable to the method of telling. As Hemingway is reported to have told A. E. Hotchner, "it was easier to write in the first person because you could involve the reader immediately. . . ."[1] Unfortunately for the critic, however, this narrative perspective also frequently disarms the reader. Especially is this true if the reader has a tendency to associate the narrator with Ernest Hemingway or to see the story as being told by a slightly older Nick Adams character. Jake Barnes is a specific character in a specific situation, and it seems to me highly important in any analysis of *The Sun Also Rises* to examine closely Jake's personality and the situation in which he finds himself. He is no traditional hero; that is clear. As the wounded man he is unable to perform as hero, even though he has the opportunity. He is, however, both the protagonist and the narrator of the novel and thus deserves the closest scrutiny.

Much of the pejorative early criticism of *The Sun Also Rises*—especially the moral criticism—makes little distinction between Jake and the other characters. Jake is frequently assumed to be one of the expatriates like Harvey Stone, Mike Campbell and Lady Brett Ashley.[2] The truth, however, is that Jake is not one of them. He is a working journalist who does, on occasion, take almost ritualistic vacation trips to Spain. Before the trip to Spain that forms the basis for this novel, he tells us that he feels very much a part of the working world: "All along the people were going to work. It felt pleasant to be going to work. I walked across the avenue and turned into my office."[3] Further, his discussions of newspaper work in the early chapters clearly indicate his competence in the field, and it is obvious that the other journalists respect him. His life is rather carefully and uncomplicatedly scheduled, and he seems to be a nucleus around which the more "restless" characters revolve. From this central position he can observe, report, and judge the activities of others and then describe the effects of the activities on him.

The most significant aspect in any consideration of Jake as a character is, of course, his impotence. F. Scott Fitzgerald, not long after the publication of *The Sun Also Rises,* wrote to Maxwell Perkins that he liked the novel but had some reservations about it.

The fiesta, the fishing trip, the minor characters were fine. The lady I didn't like, perhaps because I don't like the original. In the mutilated man I thought Ernest bit off more than can be chewn between the covers of a book, then lost his nerve a little and edited the more vitalizing details out. He has since told me that something like this happened.[4]

Fitzgerald was perhaps alluding to the problem of censorship, but there are artistic problems as well that he must have perceived. The narrative perspective in both Fitzgerald's *The Great Gatsby* and Hemingway's *The Sun Also Rises* is much the same. Nick Carraway, although not physically mutilated, is an extremely passive individual. As a representative of the "West"[5] his commentary on the East and its effect on the other Westerners and himself is central to an understanding of the novel. Nick's passivity is an especially important aspect of his personality and roughly parallels the passivity of Jake Barnes in Hemingway's novel. Both narrators are also primarily concerned with reporting the amours of other characters, although Jake is obviously the more involved of the two.

With both novels it is necessary to examine the narrator, his personality, his truthfulness, and his attitudes, since all of the action recorded is selected and arranged in terms of the writer's concept of the narrating character. What we are concerned with in *The Sun Also Rises* is a story told by a wounded—not whole—man. Thus we can not really hope for any complete solution to the problems posed by Jake.

Jake is wounded physically much as Captain Ahab's loss of leg can be seen symbolically in *Moby Dick;* both are cases of mutilation rather than castration. But, with the romantic hero passé for the naturalists, and in a novel primarily concerned with the postwar materialistic society, an Ahabian hero would be incongruous. Unlike either Ahab or his own Biblical namesake, Jacob, Jake Barnes has not been symbolically wounded by wrestling with God—he has been physically wounded in a war. Jake Barnes bears a much closer resemblance to Ishmael than to Ahab, much less concerned with trying to break through the inscrutable unreasoning mask than with trying to find a way to live in the world.

Perhaps the most important aspect of Jake's character is that, despite much critical opinion to the contrary, he is intelligent. His main purpose appears to be an attempt to come to grips with life, especially in the area of the emotions. Like many of the Nick Adams short stories which deal with Nick's discoveries about life, *The Sun Also Rises* is primarily concerned with the "education" of Jake Barnes. One of the main differences, however, between young Nick Adams and Jake Barnes is that, in most cases, Nick merely reacts emotionally to experience.[6] Things happen to him, and he suddenly becomes aware of evil or complexity, but he does not think about the concepts of good and evil. He merely reacts. Jake Barnes, in contrast, makes a conscious effort to learn about life. As he says, "Perhaps as you went along you did learn something. I did not care what it was all about. All I wanted to know was how to live in it. Maybe if you found out how to live in it you learned from that what it was all about."[7]

This passage has often been interpreted as a statement of anti-intellectualism, of the failure of the Hemingway hero to be interested in philosophical questions. Although

Jake's attitude may limit his philosophical approach, it certainly does not indicate a lack either of insight or intellectual curiosity. Jake, like Nick Carraway, reports and at the same time analyzes the experiential world and the people with whom he becomes involved. His words are more faintly reminiscent of Henry David Thoreau's statement of purpose for living at Walden.

I went to the woods because I wished to live deliberately, to front only the essential facts of life, and see if I could not learn what it had to teach, and not, when I came to die, discover that I had not lived. I did not wish to live what was not life, living is so dear; nor did I wish to practice resignation, unless it was quite necessary.[8]

There are differences, obviously. Thoreau goes on to discuss his concept of simplicity; Barnes attempts to live in the world of nature and the world of society. But both men are vitally concerned with learning about life and finding the meaning of life through living in it. Essentially, Jake Barnes observes people and society much as Thoreau observes nature. In nature Barnes finds solace rather than meaning. For meaning he looks to the statements and actions of people.

Jake examines the world initially from a rather restricted viewpoint. At the beginning of the novel he seems to have accepted a philosophy which is particularly American in its pragmatism.

You paid some way for everything that was any good. I paid my way into enough things that I liked, so that I had a good time. Either you paid by learning about them, or by experi-

ence, or by taking chances, or by money. *Enjoying living was
learning to get your money's worth and knowing when you
had it.*[9]

When Jake says that you pay for everything, he is using
"pay" much in the sense that William James uses it.[10]
Everything has its "cash value," and one determines what
to do on the basis of how much "good" one can expect to
gain by believing and acting in a certain manner. But there
is also a strain of epicureanism mixed with the pragmatism; the "good" seems to be closely related to enjoyment
or pleasure. This is also evident in Jake's commentary on
morality. "That was morality; things that made you disgusted afterward. No, that must be immorality."[11] This
statement sounds very much like the one Hemingway
makes in *Death in the Afternoon.* "So far about morals, I
know only that what is moral is what you feel good after
and what is immoral is what you feel bad after. . . ."[12]
    This appears to be an extremely simplistic treatment of
morality, but the emphasis is clearly upon an individualistic
and highly relative concept. Stressed are the physical and
emotional responses to phenomena; feeling "good" becomes pleasure in a physical and psychological sense.[13]
    But Jake Barnes is *not* Ernest Hemingway, and Jake is
more than a trifle skeptical about his own philosophy. He
recognizes that this philosophy might prove to be as silly in
the next five years as all the "other fine philosophies" he
has had. He follows his statement on morality with, "That
was a large statement. What a lot of bilge I could think up
at night."[14] For most of the novel Jake apparently operates

from this "cash nexus" type of philosophy, but I think it important that he is essentially unsure of the validity of the position, that he constantly tests it, and that he finally finds it unsatisfactory because it does not explain everything, especially in one's relationships with people.

Jake is extremely sensitive to his natural surroundings; he is also extremely sensitive to human relationships. But he is very much different from the Andersonian protagonists in *Many Marriages* and *Dark Laughter* who concentrate all of their attention upon themselves. Jake Barnes is interested in people. He is capable of having close friendships with various types of people, and he admires a number of types, from the peasants to the Count and Montoya, from Harvey Stone to Mike Campbell. But he is also aware, or becomes very much aware, that people when they are together may not get along well with one another. Perhaps the most satisfactory relationship in the novel is between Jake, Bill, and their English friend Harris on the fishing trip. In isolation, and doing what they all like to do, and without sex to complicate the relationships, the three are happy. No complex situations arise in which some people want to do things that the others do not, or in which individuals compete with one another for the satisfaction of their own needs, or where different points of view conflict. As they get on the bus Bill and Jake discuss their friend.

> "Say, wasn't that Harris nice?" Bill said.
> "I think he really did have a good time."
> "Harris? You bet he did."
> "I wish he'd come to Pamplona."[15]

But Bill seems to recognize the impossibility of transplanting the friendship to another environment. He says, "He wanted to fish." And Jake then makes an important qualification: "Yes. You couldn't tell how English would mix with each other, anyway."[16]

Part of the awareness the reader has of Jake's sensitivity results from another important aspect of his character, an extremely important one in terms of his role as narrator: Jake is almost completely honest. It is partly this honesty of Jake's, his ability to discuss the reasons for his actions that makes the reader accept his narrative. But unfortunately the reader then sometimes fails to find beneath the surface of the story as Jake tells it a double dichotomy that is part of the very structure of the novel. There is a physical or geographical emphasis which allows a contrast between the countries of France and Spain and there is a psychological emphasis which stresses significant contrasts between the characters.

The geographical dichotomy is made especially clear in Book III, which functions essentially as an epilogue. Book I (roughly sixty-seven pages) had been set in France; Book II (roughly 155 pages), primarily in Spain, and the action of Book III (twenty pages) shifts between the two countries. In the epilogue Jake reflects on his experiences in a rather conscious summing up and emphasizes the contrast between the two nations; they then become symbolic of two attitudes toward life: one essentially materialistic and sterile, the other more primitive and more virile—in a sense, almost romantic. Neither country provides an easy answer to the problem of living one's life, as Jake Barnes discovers. Life in Spain, however, finally has a more lasting effect on him.

The materialistic world of France is the easier to live in. As Jake comments,

The waiter seemed a little offended about the flowers of the Pyrenees, so I overtipped him. That made him happy. It felt comfortable to be in a country where it is so simple to make people happy. You can never tell whether a Spanish waiter will thank you. Everything is on such a clear financial basis in France. It is the simplest country to live in. No one makes things complicated by becoming your friend for any obscure reason. If you want people to like you, you have only to spend a little money. I spent a little money and the waiter liked me. He appreciated my valuable qualities. He would be glad to see me back. I would dine there again some time and he would be glad to see me, and would want me at his table. It would be a sincere liking because it would have a sound basis. I was back in France.[17]

Within the passage is a direct contrast between the waiters of France and Spain and an implied contrast between the two countries. The French waiter operates materialistically, objectively, and predictably. The Spanish waiter, it is suggested, is motivated by "obscure" reasons that make human relationships extremely difficult. Life is less complicated in France because the value systems are materialistically defined. There are no problems of abstract values and emotional responses that confuse relationships. There is irony, of course, in Jake's remark, for the important point has been developed throughout the novel that France is sterile, and this statement of contrast in the epilogue makes clear a dichotomy that has existed beneath the surface of the novel.

Jake's value system is very much like that of Count Mippipopolous, the high priest of materialism in the novel. Count Mippipopolous has a rigid system of values, and he states that the "secret" is getting to know the values. Wine and women have a strong place in his values, and he pays for his enjoyment. Love does not complicate his life because he is always in love without being emotionally involved. But Brett sagely identifies his state of being. "You haven't any values," she says. "You're dead, that's all."[18] Brett is right. Unlike the bullfighters, who live their lives "all the way up," Count Mippipopolous has quit living. It is ironically symbolic that Book I ends with a highly emotional scene between Brett and Jake, and that before going up to bed, Jake is driven home by the Count's chauffeur. Jake has just unhappily said goodbye to Brett. He has lost in his emotional life, but he receives deference from the chauffeur because he tips him. "I gave him twenty francs and he touched his cap and said: 'Good night, sir,' and drove off."[19]

The sterility of France and of both Jake's and the Count's value systems is made quite clear in a scene between Jake and Bill Gorton just after the latter has arrived in Paris.

"Here's a taxidermist's," Bill said. "Want to buy anything? Nice stuffed dog?"

"Come on," I said. "You're pie-eyed."

"Pretty nice stuffed dogs," Bill said. "Certainly brighten up your flat."

"Come on."

"Just one stuffed dog. I can take 'em or leave 'em alone. But listen, Jake. Just one stuffed dog."

"Come on."

"Mean everything in the world to you after you bought it. Simple exchange of values. You give them money. They give you a stuffed dog."[20]

One pays money for a stuffed rather than live animal. It is a simple, but meaningless, exchange of values. One notes, too, that France is the country of statues, men in stone, and most of them in some act of waving flags or raising swords. In contrast, Spain is the country of live animals— of bulls, of horses, of fish in the streams. And the men who posture with baton or sword are alive—Romero or Belmonte profiling to kill, or the policeman raising his baton in the last paragraph of the novel. This difference between countries is made even more explicit in the characterization and the description of customs.

Jake's concierge in Paris is an example of the materialistic Parisian.

Her life-work lay in the pelouse, but she kept an eye on the people of the pesage, and she took great pride in telling me which of my guests were well brought up, which were of good family, who were sportsmen, a French word pronounced with the accent on the men. The only trouble was that people who did not fall into any of these three categories were very liable to be told there was no one home, chez Barnes.[21]

It is this concierge, as a matter of fact, who, very much like the French waiter already discussed, judges Brett Ashley by the type of tip she leaves. Lady Brett alienates the concierge on her first visit to Jake's apartment, but the latter is reconciled when Brett gives her far too much of the Count's money. After the tip, the concierge says, "It was the one who was here last night. In the end I find she is very nice."[22]

In Spain, during the bus trip to the fishing location, Bill and Jake stop for a rest at a *posada*. They go inside for a drink, and then encounter the contrasting rural Spanish attitude toward tipping. "We each had an aguardiente and paid forty centimes for the two drinks. I gave the woman fifty centimes to make a tip, and she gave me back the copper piece, thinking I had misunderstood the price."[23]

Almost all of the people in France operate on the cash-value materialistic principle. This is seen especially in those people who have anything to do with the American tourists. As Jake reports,

We ate dinner at Madame Lecomte's restaurant on the far side of the island. It was crowded with Americans and we had to stand up and wait for a place. Some one had put it in the American Women's Club list as a quaint restaurant on the Paris quais as yet untouched by Americans, so we had to wait forty-five minutes for a table. Bill had eaten at the restaurant in 1918, and right after the armistice, and Madame Lecomte made a great fuss over seeing him.

"Doesn't get us a table, though," Bill said. "Grand woman, though."[24]

This kind of treatment, as contrasted to that given Jake and Bill by the hotel-keeper Montoya in Spain, emphasizes the basic satiric contrast between the two countries. Bill's recognition that the earlier friendship with Madame Lecomte has not helped at all in getting them fed is contrasted to Montoya's carefully reserving Jake's usual rooms.

From the very beginning of their journey into Spain, Jake and Bill encounter friendly people. They, as American tourists, are treated with friendliness and hospitality by the peasants on the bus. The peasants insist that the two drink from the Spanish winebags. Even commercial people are friendly. During the fiesta Jake leaves a bar to buy some wineskins. When the salesman discovers that Jake wants to use them for the purpose for which they were made, and not to sell in France, he is very considerate.

"What are you going to do? Sell them in Bayonne?"
"No. Drink out of them."
He slapped me on the back.
"Good man. Eight pesetas for the two. The lowest price."
The man who was stencilling the new ones and tossing them into a pile stopped.
"It's true," he said. "Eight pesetas is cheap."[25]

Spain is a country where materialism has not yet penetrated—at least not in certain areas. Where it has been introduced, symbolized by modern plumbing, things are beginning to change. But even in these places, the Spaniards feel guilty about their materialism.

I went out to find the woman and ask her how much the room and board was. She put her hands under her apron and looked away from me.

"*Twelve pesetas.*"

"*Why, we only paid that in Pamplona.*"

She did not say anything, just took off her glasses and wiped them on her apron.

"*That's too much,*" *I said.* "*We didn't pay more than that at a big hotel.*"

"*We've put in a bathroom.*"[26]

If Count Mippipopolous is the high priest of materialism, Montoya is the high priest of the world of "obscure" values in Spain. He has a strong sense of loyalty to those who have *aficion,* to those who have a "passion" or subjective feeling about bullfighting. As Jake says, "Those who were aficionados could always get rooms even when the hotel was full."[27] Jake also describes how Montoya is careful to hang in his office only the pictures of bullfighters who have *aficion.* He can forgive them any human weaknesses if they have the "feeling." Pictures of bullfighters without *aficion* go into his drawer and finally into the wastebasket, no matter how flattering the inscriptions. The subjective or emotional area of this relationship is indicated in Jake's description of the examination and "touching" ceremony.

When they saw that I had aficion, and there was no password, no set questions that could bring it out, rather it was a sort of oral spiritual examination with the questions always a little on the defensive and never apparent, there was this same embarrassed putting the hand on the shoulder, or a "Buen hombre." But nearly always there was the actual touching. It seemed as though they wanted to touch you to make it certain.[28]

Montoya, as one of the "touchers," represents this traditional and subjective area of experience, and he is in direct
contrast to Count Mippipopolous and the rest of the Parisian materialists.

The contrast between France and Spain is most highly
developed in the disparity between the national "sports" of
the two countries. The emphasis that Hemingway places
on bullfighting is easily recognized through Jake Barnes'
interest in it and his feeling for it. We see something of the
traditional and ritualistic aspects of the bullfight in Jake's
description. We also note his admiration for the meaningfulness of the forms of the bullfight and of the passes, and
the recognition that each *torero* tests his integrity each
time he encounters the bull. Furthermore, the *torero* faces
death, not as the man who is killed during the unloading
and running of the bulls, but in an art form where each act
has not only beauty but meaning. The whole ceremony,
then, is the antithesis of the meaningless world Jake Barnes
and his friends live in. This is the "sport" of Spain. Jake
Barnes is one of the initiated who have *aficion,* who have
the subjective feeling about what goes on in the bullring,
and who understand the deeper meanings behind the bullfight. He does not react emotionally only, like those who
fail to give Juan Belmonte his due, but can appreciate artistically both the worth of the young Romero and the great
dignity of Belmonte in this "sport" which is played always
in the face of death.

Bicycle racing, the contrasting sport of France, is another
thing. Having lunch with the team manager of one of the
bicycle manufacturers, Jake is told that the Tour de France

is "the greatest sporting event in the world."[29] But there is no dignity in bicycle racing. It is, if it can be called such, a materialistic sport, where everything important can be taken care of, and where there is very little of the element of chance. As Jake reports, "[The bicycle riders] did not take the race seriously except among themselves. They had raced among themselves so often that it did not make much difference who won. Especially in a foreign country. The money could be arranged."[30]

There is neither the dignity nor the heavy masculinity of the bullfighter in the picture of the bicycle racers. The racers have a following of French girls with "Rue de Faubourg Montmartre chic" who seem to be almost community property, for Jake cannot make out which girl belongs to which racer. The racers whisper jokes they think the girls should not hear, and then will not repeat them. They are quite unlike Romero, who remains with his cuadrilla apart from society until the point when he quite aggressively approaches Brett. He is so direct that Jake can analyze his every move and correctly interprets his glance that indicates things are "understood." Nor are the bicycle racers exposed, as Romero is, to a horn wound or fatality. Bicycle racing does not involve the potentially tragic element of a direct confrontation with death. The leader of the bicycle racers ridiculously has an attack of boils which forces him to sit on the small of his back. He blushes when one of the girls hears him tell how he is going to ride the next day with the air touching his boils. These are sportsmen, not men. Jake makes no direct comparison of bicycle racing to the bullfight, but he does make one ironic comment that makes the point beautifully. "The Spaniards, they [the French] said, did not know how to pedal."[31] The mechanical act of pedalling is completely unimportant in contrast to the traditions and meaningful forms of the bullfight. Jake, who travels annually from one country to another as though on a religious pilgrimage, and who watches almost all of the preliminary activities as well as the bullfight itself, does not bother to watch the bicycle racers start the next morning. In fact, he indicates to the team manager that he would prefer not to be wakened for the event.

The meaninglessness and sterility of life in Paris or in France becomes evident in the implicit comparison to Spain. The meaninglessness caused by the disruption of social patterns resulting from the war is symbolized most effectively in the geographical or national contrast by two passages illustrating the present condition of the two countries. France is a far more modern and progressive country. The concept of change is evident, and Bill Gorton, though he loves the city and is glad to be back, takes a dim view of one of the changes.

We walked along under the trees that grew out over the river on the Quai d'Orléans side of the island. Across the river were the broken walls of old houses that were being torn down.
   "They're going to cut a street through."
   "They would," Bill said.[32]

In contrast, when Jake returns to Spain, he finds almost everything the way he remembers it. Symbolically, the

Ayuntamiento is the center of the old civilization, unchanging, the home of the history of the town.

I went to the Ayuntamiento and found the old gentleman who subscribes for the bull-fight tickets for me every year, and he had gotten the money I sent him from Paris and renewed my subscriptions, so that was all set. He was the archivist, and all the archives of the town were in his office. That has nothing to do with the story. Anyway, his office had a green baize door and a big wooden door, and when I went out I left him sitting among the archives that covered all the walls, and I shut both the doors, and as I went out of the building into the street the porter stopped me to brush off my coat.

"You must have been in a motor-car," he said.

The back of the collar and the upper part of the shoulders were gray with dust.[33]

The description is obviously important. Here is the seat of a society, the society of Spain. From here Jake goes to the cathedral to pray, and becomes disappointed with himself for being such a bad Catholic. It is interesting, however, that when praying for the bullfighters, he treats them much as Montoya treats their pictures, "[praying] separately for the ones I liked, and lumping all the rest. . . ."[34] Further, he begins to think about making money, and this reminds him of Count Mippipopolous. The most important quality of the description of the Ayuntamiento, however, is that the dust that Jake had accumulated on his coat during the drive from Bayonne becomes symbolic of the Spanish earth. In the epilogue Jake arrives at San Sebastian and wistfully makes a symbolic gesture to the dust of

Spain. "At the hotel I paid the driver and gave him a tip. The car was powdered with dust. I rubbed the rodcase through the dust. It seemed the last thing that connected me with Spain and the fiesta."[35]

Spain, then, is at the center of tradition and represents the old truths, the old concepts, the old ways. France is the new way, the materialistic direction, the country of twentieth-century change. The movement between the two countries is especially important in terms of a parallel development in the cast of characters. The novel begins in France, where there are no meaningful rituals and, of course, no heroes. Jake's coterie of friends intrude upon his planned vacation with Bill Gorton and enter into the land of meaning. After Jake and Bill return from their fishing trip in the mountains the stage is set for the representatives of the materialistic world to make their impact on the world of tradition. Although Jake at first chooses to remain loyal to his Paris friends, the final victory is won by Romero, the representative of Spain. He wins because this is the land of tradition, a land where the hero may still live. And the victory of the hero has a strong effect on Jake Barnes. The geographical movement in the novel parallels and enforces the gradual shift in emphasis from one character to another.

For as Jake tells the story, he gradually shifts his focus. He begins his narration with a description of Cohn; the first book is primarily devoted to Cohn and Brett and himself. In the second book emphasis is transferred from Cohn and Brett to Mike and Brett and finally to Romero and Brett. Romero completely replaces the other suitors by the end of Book II. In Book III, which serves as an epilogue, Jake is left alone, but returns to Spain to rescue Brett.

Both Earl Rovit[36] and Mark Spilka[37] make the interesting point that Cohn functions essentially as Jake's "double." What they neglect, however, is that Cohn represents only Jake's passive and romantic side when there is still another important side to be considered. Jake is a more complex character than he seems to be. He is the only character in the novel, with the possible exception of Bill Gorton, who is at home in both of the environments. He lives a comfortable, fairly controlled life in France until Brett Ashley interferes, and he is equally comfortable and at home in Spain until once again Lady Brett and all of his friends intrude. It should be remembered that Jake has made the trip to Spain a number of times. He is familiar with bullfighting, has been recognized as having *aficion,* and has never broken the rules of loyalty—until, of course, he arranges the meeting between Romero and Brett.

Perhaps the reason for his disloyalty can be seen in a comparison of the two aspects of his personality represented by Cohn and Romero. If we use the sociological terminology of David Riesman's *The Lonely Crowd,* these differences can perhaps be clarified. Robert Cohn might be classified as a man who might well use his tradition-directed background, but who has no basic "inner-direction" for coping with the value-less "other-directed" post-war society in which he finds himself. Cohn is Jewish, but he has broken from the traditional Jewish way of life. He is, in fact, ashamed of his Jewish background. He learned to box to counteract a feeling of inferiority when he was treated as a Jew. And he received a "strange sort of satisfaction" at having his nose flattened. But with the Jewish tradition to fall back on, Cohn takes a different course. He becomes an editor and then a novelist. Like an insect who points his feelers out into the world and then responds to what it feels, he is constantly putting out his own antennae. He has never had set in motion the "internal gyroscope" of an inner-directed man. He is completely unable to make up his mind about anything until he falls in love. Having broken from his tradition, and with no strong sense of himself, he is as empty as a man can be. He is completely dominated by Frances, or would be except for what Jake would later call his hard, stubborn, Jewish streak, which is the only strength he has. Later, he is dominated by Lady Brett, but this time because he is completely overpowered by his infatuation for her. As Jake points out, Cohn gets his romantic ideas from very impractical books. He is extremely conscious of his failure to live, and even speaks to Jake about it.

When Jake asks him if he has had any fun the night before, Cohn gives a well-qualified answer. "No, I don't think so."[38] This is the same type of reaction evidenced in the one Spanish peasant on the bus ride who had been to America and whose traditions had been confused. When asked if he likes the bullfight, he says, "Yes. I guess I like them."[39]

Cohn is much closer than Jake to the Anderson type of "wounded" hero that Hemingway had satirized in *The Torrents of Spring*. He is self-interested, with a tendency toward emotionalism, and with a strong belief that a ro-

mantic interest with the right woman in the right environment is what he needs in order to "live." He believes that a
change of environment will solve his problems when he
is, like an Anderson hero, trying to escape from one woman
to another. Just as he believes that he can find "life" in
romantic South America, he also believes that his sexual
interlude with Brett is a great love, and thus allows himself
to be destroyed by her. In this respect, as Spilka has pointed
out, he is much like Jake Barnes in the early part of the
novel, who believes that if he were not physically wounded
he would be able to provide Brett with all of the qualities
necessary for her happiness.

The major difference between the two men is in the
nature of the wound. Cohn is psychologically wounded,
while Jake is physically wounded. Jake has been unmanned
by the war, although left with all of his masculine drives.
He is not self-centered, as Cohn is, and his passivity is
largely a device that he has used in order, as he says, to keep
from making trouble. Though he loves Brett and is dominated by her for a large part of the novel, he is finally able
to recognize her emotional limitations. As he says, "I suppose she only wanted what she couldn't have."[40] As a
wounded man, we do not expect heroic activity from Jake,
especially on a physical level. But we do expect him to act
with integrity. In the one important decision he has to
make in the novel, he fails.

The most significant "action" in the novel involves Jake's
choice of whether or not to introduce Brett to Romero.
Strangely enough, Jake as narrator tells us very little about
the reasons for this decision, which is the crucial moral

action in the novel. Thus, what he has chosen to tell us about Spain and his recapitulation of the differences between France and Spain become exceptionally important to an understanding of Jake Barnes and of the novel itself.

When Jake is not under pressure, he makes the "right" decision in terms of his loyalty to Montoya, bullfighting, and the subjective, traditional way of life. Montoya asks his advice after Romero has been invited to the American ambassador's suite at the Grand Hotel. Jake tells Montoya not to deliver the message to Romero, and they talk about the dangers to the career of the young torero. The major danger seems to be older women who collect bullfighters. In his advice to Montoya, Jake is loyal to the bullfight and to all that it represents in the novel.

But when Lady Brett asks for Jake's help in meeting Romero, Jake lacks the integrity to deny her wishes. He becomes, as Cohn later calls him, a "pimp," and is disloyal to those things that he has respected. It is at this point in the novel that Jake has the opportunity to act with integrity, and it is at this point in the novel that he fails. He refuses the role of the hero.

His failure, however, is only a partial failure, because his reasons for sending Brett away with Romero are complex. For one thing, he is getting even with Cohn for running away with Brett, and it is rather easy to trace the change from pity toward Cohn at the beginning of the novel to hostility after his discovery that Cohn and Brett have been away together. As he confesses to Brett, "I'm not sorry for him. I hate him, myself."[41] But in his act of disloyalty he is, at the same time, destroying that part of himself that, as Rovit and Spilka suggest, Cohn represents. Even more important, he is replacing Cohn with another figure and another part of himself, the masculine and heroic side that has been powerless and inactive since his wound. Finally, he may even by trying to punish and destroy the bitch goddess, the tempting sorceress, by mating her with a surrogate lover, Romero.

Jake Barnes is not totally passive; rather, he has elements of strength and areas of belief that he is unable to maintain in the face of human conflicts and a changing world. Between the idea of how he should act and the reality of how he does falls the shadow of his wound. He is, like his namesake, the man with the hollow "thigh." But he is just as much Romero on one side of his character as he is Cohn on the other. Romero becomes the symbol for what he could have been had he not been wounded and had there been no twentieth-century moral revolution in the material world. Both Jake and Romero have *aficion,* and Jake understands Romero's motives in the bullring as though he *were* Romero. They both have the same attitudes toward honor. When Mike tells Jake the story about Romero's defeat of Cohn through Romero's refusal to be defeated (Romero kept trying to hit Cohn and refused to shake his hand), we recognize that this is the way Jake would have acted had he been able. After Jake has sent Brett off with Romero, for example, he has far more courage than he has had previously. Instead of backing away from trouble, as he had when Cohn once threatened to hit him for his remarks about Brett, Jake now actually starts a fight.

I swung at him and he ducked. I saw his face duck sideways
in the light. He hit me and I sat down on the pavement. As I
started to get on my feet he hit me twice. I went down backward under a table. I tried to get up and felt I did not have
any legs. I felt I must get on my feet and try and hit him.[42]

But Jake is unable to get up. His attitude, however, is the
same as Romero's, and is very unlike Mike's who says. "He
didn't knock me out. I just lay there." Even more important, perhaps, is the feeling Jake has about not accepting
Cohn's apology. Again he wishes to act as Romero has
acted. Jake returns to the hotel, and Bill tells him to go see
Cohn. Jake says, "The hell with him," but Bill insists that
he go. Jake climbs another flight of stairs, knocks on Cohn's
door, and identifies himself as "Barnes," not "Jake." He at
first refuses to allow Cohn to call him by his first name.
Then he is reminded once more that this was how he had
felt when he had come home from a football game after
being hit in the head. His immediate reaction to the concept of "home" is that he suddenly wants a "deep, hot bath,
to lie back in." He refuses to forgive Cohn, reminds him
that he had called him a pimp and then thinks, "I did not
care. I wanted a hot bath. I wanted a hot bath in deep
water."[43]

As he finds out later he wishes to react very much like
Romero acted after his physical defeat by Cohn; but he is
incapable. He is unable to face the complexity of the world,
is unable to live by the code that Romero uses to preserve
his integrity. Instead, he decides that he does not really

care and symbolically wishes to retire from the world into an obviously symbolic womb.

The contrast between the actions of Jake and Romero emphasizes the unheroic nature of Jake as protagonist. Romero is the hero, the bullfighter who lives his life "all the way up." He lives according to his traditions, even refusing to speak English any more than absolutely necessary because bullfighters should not know English. He preserves his integrity despite the physical punishment he receives from Cohn. Then he erases the whole incident, as Jake realizes, by his performance in the traditional ritual of the bullfight. Like the true hero, Romero faces every trial successfully. He even temporarily conquers the temptress, a feat that none of the other males has been able to accomplish. He can conquer because he is what might be called the "tradition-directed" hero.

Life is far more simple for Romero than for the expatriates. Living the restricted life of a bullfighter with his cuadrilla, he has fewer choices to make. He must work his own individuality into the definitely traditionalized ritual of the bullfight. He is presented at each corrida with a certain number of bulls to kill ritualistically—bulls which he has not been allowed to choose, although his manager might help in the selection. Most important, his profession is his way of life, and he lives within it. It includes a code of honor that he may respect and live by. It is not the audience that is to be pleased at each corrida. As Jake understands, Romero does it for himself. He does not, like the "other-directed" individual, do things to please others and to justify himself in their terms. Nor does his older counterpart, Belmonte.

Carlos Baker overlooks the one point that Jake's description of Juan Belmonte serves in the novel. Belmonte, too, is a bullfighter who lives his life "all the way up." He is an old Romero whose popularity has diminished, but who maintains at least some degree of his old integrity. As Jake explains, Belmonte is careful about the selection of bulls and has lost his belief in the "great moments" of bullfighting. But unlike the inactive Count Mippipopolous, Belmonte continues to test himself despite his illness and thus he preserves some of his dignity and integrity. He is a sick man, in constant pain, but he does not allow the reaction of the crowd to destroy his composure. Worst of all, he is the mythological hero who cannot at his age—or could not, even in his best years, Jake tells us—do the things the crowd now expects of him. Jake's description of Belmonte in the ring shows more contempt for the crowd than for Belmonte. At the end of the passage, Belmonte, untouched by the crowd, goes back to take his part in the ritual.

Also Belmonte imposed conditions and insisted that his bulls should not be too large, nor too dangerously armed with horns, and so the element that was necessary to give the sensation of tragedy was not there, and the public, who wanted three times as much from Belmonte, who was sick with a fistula, as Belmonte had ever been able to give, felt defrauded and cheated, and Belmonte's jaw came further out in contempt, and his face turned yellower, and he moved with greater difficulty as his pain increased, and finally the crowd were actively against him, and he was utterly contemptuous and indifferent. He had meant to have a great afternoon, and instead it was an afternoon of sneers, shouted insults, and finally a volley of cushions and pieces of bread and vegetables, thrown down at him in the plaza where he had his greatest triumphs. His jaw only went further out. Sometimes he turned to smile that toothed, long-jawed, lipless smile when he was called something particularly insulting, and always the pain that any movement produced grew stronger and stronger, until finally his yellow face was parchment color, and after his second bull was dead and the throwing of bread and cushions was over, after he had saluted the President with the same wolf-jawed smile and contemptuous eyes, and handed his sword over the barrera to be wiped, and put back in its case, he passed through into the collejon and leaned on the barrera below us, his head on his arms, not seeing, not hearing anything, only going through his pain. When he looked up, finally, he asked for a drink of water. He swallowed a little, rinsed his mouth, spat the water, took his cape, and went back into the ring.[44]

Belmonte, as seen here, is one of the undefeated. In a sense his dignity is unsurpassed even by Romero.

There is the same essential difference, then, between Belmonte and Cohn that there is between Romero and Cohn. Both Romero and Belmonte refuse to accept defeat, but Cohn collapses completely after Brett has left and he has taken out his spite on Jake. He lies with his face to the wall, cries, and begs for both forgiveness and sympathy. Finally, he leaves the scene of the fiesta before the last act, sneaking out almost unobserved.

It is apparently the bullfighter, then, who serves as the best example of how one can face life. Here in the Romero-Belmonte figure is the only character, or combination of characters, who successfully resists all of the forces imposed on him from the outside world. In Romero's refusal to be defeated by physical punishment at the hands of Cohn and, more important, to be dominated by Lady Brett Ashley is found the important lesson of the concepts of honor and integrity that are based in a traditional way of life and are given solidity by it.

Thus, when Jake deliberates whether to introduce Brett to Romero and later to deliver her to him, he is not only choosing between his loyalties to materialism represented by his friends from France and those traditional values represented by Spain and Montoya, he is also choosing between two aspects of his own personality. Unconsciously, he is delivering Brett to his own better self and destroying the Cohn relationship and that part of himself that is passive. Even more, he may be unconsciously trying to punish Lady Brett by introducing her to the dominant male figure—the hero he cannot be.[45]

Lady Brett Ashley has dominated all of the males. She is very much like the street vendor's girl attendant who is described at the beginning of Chapter V, immediately after the chapter devoted to Brett and Jake's relationship. "I passed the man with the jumping frogs and the man with the boxer toys. I stepped aside to avoid walking into the thread with which his girl assistant manipulated the boxers. She was standing looking away, the thread in her folded hands."[46] Although Brett becomes a goddess of the fiesta, she is a false goddess. She is a temptress who destroys, and then hates those, like Cohn, who suffer from her destruction.

Jake, too, comes to hate Cohn. "I'm not sorry for him. I hate him, myself," he says, before Brett tells him about her love for Romero. After Jake warns her that she should not become involved with Romero, he becomes suddenly angry. They find Romero in the bar and converse while they wait for him to join them.

> "I've always done just what I wanted."
> "I know."
> "I do feel such a bitch."
> "Well," I said.
> "My God!" said Brett, "the things a woman goes through."
> "Yes?"[47]

Jake then joins his other friends and fights with Cohn. After the fight he seems to change in his attitude toward Brett. Instead of showing his anger and jealousy, he is quite sympathetic and helpful to her. He seems to enjoy Romero's conquest of the bull as much as Brett does, and his narration concentrates all the attention upon Romero and the older bullfighter Belmonte. After the bullfight he gets drunk on absinthe that tastes "pleasantly bitter." On this last night of the fiesta, he is drunker than he has ever remembered being.

This is a fitting conclusion to the action of the novel. The hero has departed with what he thinks to be the goddess. If this were a romantic novel, it would end here, or Jake would go on to tell an adapted version of the heroic myth, which traditionally ends in the marriage of the hero and the goddess.[48] Lady Brett, however, will not play the role of goddess. She is, as Robert Lewis has recognized, the woman in Ecclesiastes whose "heart is snares and nets."[49] She is the temptress, and though Romero is the traditional hero, he is not the protagonist of the novel. Thus, the epilogue is concerned with the result of the union of the hero and the temptress and the effects of the union on the narrator. Of major significance in the epilogue is the fact that the heroic figure has replaced the passive figure and that this replacement affects Jake Barnes' attitude toward Lady Brett.[50] In the beginning of the epilogue Jake makes a reluctant and ironic acceptance of France, but only because he is a wounded man. He rationalizes that France is an easy country to live in. It is a country where loyalties do not conflict and where one's integrity is thus not always being tested. There is, however, something shameful about his choice.

As his attitude toward her changes in this last book nothing seems shameful any longer in his relation to Brett. At the beginning of the novel Jake is so emotionally disturbed by Brett that he cannot sleep. When they meet at the dance, he wants to take her away immediately. They are both disturbed at his inability to consummate their love, and Jake is in almost a constant state of torment. On one occasion Brett seems able to provide him with some makeshift physical release, but there is usually none at all. While they are in Spain at the fiesta, Jake is still under her control, and he is very upset when Brett forces him to introduce her to Romero. He witnesses Romero's triumph and then leaves for San Sebastian where he has time to think and to swim. It is immediately after his immersion that he receives the "S.O.S." telegram from Brett and answers it. His initial reaction is one of self-contempt. "That seemed to handle it. That was it. Send a girl off with one man. Introduce her to another to go off with him. Now go and bring her back. And sign the wire with love. That was it all right. I went to lunch."[51]

It has not been as simple as this, of course. Jake reports the action without commenting on his own emotional involvement. He has punished both Cohn and Brett for their escapade, and he has exposed Brett to the traditional masculine hero who has wiped out her experience with Cohn. Jake has also had time for some reflection, and his attitude toward Brett is quite different when he returns to Spain. By the time he finds her in Madrid, he is in almost complete control of himself. His attitude toward Brett is fatherly, if not actually condescending. He kisses her, but notices that her mind is on something else. He comforts her rather than allowing her to comfort him. His control is not easy to maintain. The effort is obviously difficult, and can be seen in his response to her questions, with clipped answers that steer away from any involvement. She seems to sense this and is slightly helpful when she tells him he does not have to get drunk. Later in the cab he puts his arm around her, but there is no longer the frantic need that he had previously felt. The two cab scenes, one at the beginning of the novel and one at the end, make some rather nice distinctions. In the first,

Brett was leaning back in the corner, her eyes closed. I got in and sat beside her. The cab started with a jerk.

"Oh, darling, I've been so miserable," Brett said.

The taxi went up the hill. . . . The street was dark again

and I kissed her. Our lips were tight together and then she turned away and pressed against the corner of the seat, as far away as she could get. Her head was down.

"Don't touch me," she said. "Please don't touch me."[52]

But at the end, when Jake gets in beside Brett,

. . . I settled back. Brett moved close to me. We sat close against each other. I put my arm around her and she rested against me comfortably. . . .

"Oh, Jake," Brett said, "we could have had such a damned good time together."

Ahead was a mounted policeman in khaki directing traffic. He raised his baton. The car slowed suddenly pressing Brett against me.

"Yes," I said. "Isn't it pretty to think so?"[53]

The imagery in the first cab scene is dark. It is night. The second scene takes place in the brightness of the sun. Such symbolism is slightly ambiguous, however. It might be interpreted as a continuation of the day-night difference of two different worlds, more prevalent in *A Farewell to Arms,* but certainly a part of *The Sun Also Rises;* and it could also indicate the clarity with which Jake is finally able to view the situation, in keeping with other passages in the novel where light and truth seem to be synonymous, as at the bullfight. But the most important distinctions to be made are less ambiguous.

In the first passage, the cab starts; in the second, it stops. In the first, the two are tense with emotion and Brett breaks away from him after the kiss; in the second she moves closer to him and then sits "comfortably" with his arm around her. The policeman's raised baton reminds him at once of both his own incapacity and, equally important, Brett's selfishness and lack of understanding. What has become clear to Jake from the slight victory he has gained through Romero is the recognition that Brett could never become a woman even if he were not wounded. She would not let her hair grow for Romero because of her vanity; she could not destroy Romero, and neither could she change for him. Psychologically, she can no more be a woman than Jake can be a man. His ironic reply, "Isn't it pretty to think so" to Brett's "we could have had such a damned good time together" brings the novel full circle, for Jake had earlier known but could not accept the fact that the only reason she wanted him was because she could not have him. There is no more hope now than at the beginning of the novel, but Jake is apparently far more resigned to his condition. He is dedicated, after watching Romero's conquest, to preserving himself against the forces of the temptress. Jake learns to accept the inevitable, as preached in Ecclesiastes, that "All is vanity and vexation of spirit."

The Sun Also Rises, then, is essentially a satire on mankind, much as Ecclesiastes can be looked at as a satire on the vanity of human attempts to find meaning in life. The novel falls into the category of those works on the "Vanity of Human Wishes" theme. Jake looks at all experience and finds it lacking. There are no simple answers for the individual— especially the wounded man—and no code is going to eliminate the problems and perplexities of human relationships in a traditionless world, although it would be pretty to think so. The materialistic world of France is bereft of meaning, and the world of Spain, with its obscure value system and its rigid traditional code is too demanding for the wounded man. Jake finds some solace in nature, however, and he has learned something about integrity from the heroic Romero-Belmonte figure in contrast to the "lost" expatriates. Jake is no hero, but he has learned something from the hero figure—a contempt for the crowd and a certain indifference to his own fate. There are to be no more illusions. And with this knowledge comes a certain compassion for Lady Brett and a recognition of the need for restraint in his association with her. Thoreau had said that he did not want to practice resignation "unless it was quite necessary." Jake Barnes, the wounded man in the rapidly changing traditionless and heroless twentieth century, seems to find it necessary.

III

A FARE-
WELL TO
ARMS:

The Guilt-Ridden Anti-HERO

DESPITE MALCOLM COWLEY's frequently quoted statement about the similarities between Hemingway and the great romantics,[1] most of the criticism of *A Farewell to Arms* has assumed that it is primarily a naturalistic novel with either the young Ernest Hemingway or the Nick Adams figure as the protagonist. Typical of such criticism is George Snell's remark that *"A Farewell to Arms . . .* might chronologically be taken to precede *The Sun Also Rises,* for it is a history of Jake Barnes in an earlier incarnation, a morally wounded young man in the midst of war, in love with a somewhat less bitchy Lady Brett, named Catherine."[2]

Overlooking this rather inane commentary on Catherine (although it is an attitude perpetuated in Sheridan Baker's *Ernest Hemingway*[3]), Snell's statement once again suggests the popular concept of a progressive Hemingway hero. Yet neither Jake Barnes nor Frederic Henry is a hero; they are, in fact, both anti-heroes, but the forces that act upon them to cause their lack of heroism differ significantly. Although both protagonists are essentially passive, they are different in character and they are different as narrators.

One of the most important differences between the protagonists of the two novels is the way in which each reports his story. Jake is almost always honest in his recapitulation of events. He is often self-effacing, and he seldom attempts to justify his own actions by blaming the rest of the world or the universe. In contrast, Frederic Henry has a strong tendency to rationalize every action, especially those which make him feel guilty. He is willing to blame the world or the system or fate, but seldom himself. In *The Catcher in The Rye*,[4] J. D. Salinger has his sensitive adolescent say some rather perceptive things about the protagonist of *A Farewell to Arms*. Holden is discussing his brother's attitude about war, and he wonders how D. B. can espouse a hatred for war when, at the same time, he likes *A Farewell to Arms*. Holden finds it especially difficult to understand how D. B. can think that Lieutenant Henry is a nice guy, for Holden sees him as being insincere. Finally, Salinger's protagonist compares the Hemingway novel with a book by Ring Lardner and Fitzgerald's *The Great Gatsby*. Holden, of course, has his own problems with insincerity. His own narration attempts to disguise his failures through an attack on others, and he is particularly alert to this method when others use it. Thus he can attack Hemingway's novel and protagonist as phonies—in his evaluation of Lieutenant Henry, Holden may be right.

Although each story is told in the first-person, the narrative technique Hemingway used in the World War I novel is significantly different from the one used in *The Sun Also Rises*. In *The Sun Also Rises* there is a strong sense of immediacy, as though Jake had told the story within a week or two after his meeting with Brett in Madrid. Further, this sense of immediacy is made more striking by the unity of time in the novel. Everything, except the recounting of Cohn's past, is treated in a chronological sequence which is easy to follow and which covers a matter of only a few weeks. Sequence is broken in *A Farewell to Arms,* and rather carefully. Although there is after the first chapter a sequential, chronological movement to the action of the novel, the first chapter itself is like a prologue that occurs a year before the second chapter starts. From the outset, then, we have the feeling that the narrator is reflecting upon an experience which took place long enough ago for him to telescope the two years together. Although the story is told with a strong sense of the immediacy of the events themselves, there are frequent references to a time lapse, as in the beginning of Chapter XVIII. "We had a lovely time that summer. When I could go out we rode in a carriage in the park. I remember the carriage, the horse going slowly, and up ahead the back of the driver with his varnished high hat, and Catherine Barkley sitting beside me."[5] Again, at the beginning of Chapter XXXVIII, there is a reminder that the story is being told in retrospect. "That fall the snow came very late. We lived in a brown wooden house in the pine trees on the side of the mountain and at night there was frost so that there was thin ice over the water in the two pitchers on the dresser in the morning."[6]

These introductory elements establish the narrator's position, that of a man looking nostalgically at the past. We do not know precisely from what distance he is recalling the events, but we do know that he has had time to evaluate his experience. The effect of the time lapse is heightened even more in the original version of the conclusion of the novel which makes it clear, through the recapitulation of what had happened to some of the characters, that the narrator is looking back on the experience after almost ten years:

> I could tell how Rinaldi was cured of the syphilis and lived to find that the technic learned in wartime surgery is not of much practical use in peace. I could tell how the priest in our mess lived to be a priest in Italy under Fascism. I could tell how Ettore became a Fascist and the part he took in that organization. I could tell how Piani got to be a taxi-driver in New York and what sort of a singer Simmons became. Many things have happened.[7]

This version results in an epilogue-like tone which was de-emphasized in the final printed version. In the original ending, the emphasis is not on the immediate shock of Catherine's death, but on Frederic Henry's generalized philosophical concepts of the death of the individual as opposed to the continuum of life on the earth. "Everything blunts and the world keeps on. It never stops. It only stops for you. Some of it stops while you are still alive. The rest goes on and you go on with it."[8]

What Hemingway gained artistically in his decision to

discard the philosophical conclusion was the sense of the immediate emotional impact of Catherine's death on his narrator—and on the reader. What he lost, however, was the reflective quality of the original conclusion, a quality much like that of the original ending, say, of Dickens' *Great Expectations.* He also lost by his revision the frame-like structure of an epilogue which balanced the prologue. Most important, however, is that the conclusion as it finally appeared concentrates upon the death scene and Frederic's response so that the reader is disarmed into seeing the narrator as Frederic tends to view himself—a victim of circumstances, of a hostile social structure, and of an indifferent universe.

With the epilogue-like ending we may well have expected Frederic Henry to have seen after a period of ten years his own involvement and his own guilt in what took place, much as Pip in *Great Expectations* can look back in the final chapter and discuss his own guilt. In the original conclusion to *A Farewell to Arms* there is at least a hint of an indirect self-analysis by Frederic when he states that he has been "going on with the rest of my life—which has gone on and seems likely to go on for a long time."[9] As Frederic has already pointed out, the world "kills the very good and the very gentle and the very brave impartially. If you are none of these you can be sure it will kill you too but there will be no special hurry."[10] He thus identifies himself as one of those the world is not in a hurry to kill, and thus as not one of the very good, the very gentle, or the very brave. He is not, then, one of the heroes. There is no such self-indictment evident in the published ending, and the lack of it disguises but does not alter this part of the novel's emphasis. Hemingway departs from the nineteenth-century novelist's tendency to point up a "message" at the end of the novel, or to explain its meaning. As a result, the whole novel must be examined in order to find the narrator's relation to the material he reports.

The tone of Frederic Henry's story is one of disillusionment and, according to Maurice Shroder, disillusionment is one of the chief characteristics of the type of novel which is concerned with the anti-hero or unheroic hero. Shroder goes on to explain

that the novelist is the eiron, while his protagonist (the "imaginist," the romance sensibility in a real world) is an alazon who learns, through disillusionment, that he is not a hero after all. Unlike the inflationary novelist, who advertises his characters (if not himself), the deflationary novelist, the ironic author, appears to allow his characters to magnify themselves, but is in reality subtly and silently reducing them to their actual stature.[11]

Hemingway uses the ironic approach in allowing Frederic Henry to present his own story. *A Farewell to Arms* is, in Shroder's terms, a deflationary novel. Although the reader is aware that Frederic Henry is a potential hero engaged in military action, Frederic Henry never performs an act of heroism. The original ending of the novel made it clear that Frederic Henry was no hero; the final version, to use Shroder's description, allows us to see that Frederic Henry is in reality "subtly and silently" reduced to his actual stature.

One of the primary concerns in evaluating this novel is trying to determine the motivations for Henry's actions and, specifically, the reasons for his failure to act heroically. As with Jake Barnes, there is a discrepancy between the idea, or the ideal, and the reality, but the shadow that falls between them in *A Farewell to Arms* is caused not only by the external world, which the narrator frequently blames, but also by the very powerful basic human drives of sex and self-preservation.

Like other naturalistic novelists, the early Hemingway is highly concerned with the psychological forces that overpower the individual from within. An evaluation of Lt. Henry's actions and the motivations for his actions illustrates that he fails to act heroically because he is unable to cope with these forces and thus fails both Catherine and himself. There are at least two important passages in the novel which deserve close analysis because they contain the germ of Frederic Henry's anti-heroism. The first of these must be viewed in terms of Frederic's personality as it is presented before the incident takes place and also in terms of his attitude toward the war.

Frederic Henry is primarily a democratic, protestant individual who is considerate of servants and his men, is deferential to others, especially older people, and who has respect for religion even though he is not religious. He has not yet determined just what he can believe in. Like Jake Barnes, he sees a difference between the night and the day, and has trouble deciding between the objective and the subjective areas of experience. But two other qualities should be mentioned. He is extremely selfish; thus he is unable to love. And he is not truly brave.

We know essentially nothing about Frederic Henry's reasons for joining the Italian Army, except that he was in Italy studying architecture when the war broke out and he could speak Italian. However, certain bitter passages like the one that begins "I was always embarrassed by the words sacred, glorious, and sacrifice and the expression in vain" lead one to believe that he may have enlisted in a burst of enthusiasm that he has since regretted. Every incident at the beginning of the novel indicates that the young Frederic Henry is less sympathetic with the war than with the human beings who are involved in it. He is sympathetic with the feelings and attitudes of his ambulance drivers, even when they speak treason. When he sees a lone soldier by the side of the road and learns that the man has been to Pittsburgh and that he has thrown away his truss, Lieutenant Henry offers to help him get sent to the rear. Ostensibly he does not like the war and wishes it were over, even though he at first has no fear that he will be killed in it. After he is wounded, however, he knows that he can be killed. This knowledge in no way makes him any more enthusiastic about the war. Thus the reader is surprised at some of Frederic Henry's actions. For example, Frederic is far more impressed with the war hero Ettore than is Catherine, and when Frederic purchases a pistol just before leaving for the front, he does it with a flourish in front of Catherine. He is showing off, much as Ettore would. Frederic Henry plays the role of the soldier hero at times, but he does not play it well.

He is particularly inept in his handling of the retreat orders. He allows his men three hours for sleep after everyone else has left. Then they eat a leisurely meal and finally join the column of trucks and wagons in the retreat. Disturbed by the slowness of the retreat column, Frederic Henry decides to leave the main group and take one of the small country roads. He reasons that

No one knew where the Austrians were nor how things were going but I was certain that if the rain should stop and planes come over and get to work on that column that it would be all over. All that was needed was for a few men to leave their trucks or a few horses to be killed to tie up completely the movement on the road.[12]

The rain does stop, but at the same time they hear the planes bombing the retreat column on the main road, they become helplessly stuck in a muddy country road. The two sergeants who have been riding with them and whom Frederic Henry has allowed to stay because they can be used "to push" are impatient to be moving. They have lost confidence in him because he has told them he does not know where the road leads and he has allowed his men to dally at a farmhouse where they pause for food. Now, with the lead ambulance stuck up to its differential, they begin to walk away. Lieutenant Henry, not a combat soldier but an ambulance officer, goes after them.

"Come on," I said. "Cut some brush."

"We have to go," one said.

"Get busy," I said, "and cut brush."

"We have to go," one said. The other said nothing. They were in a hurry to start. They would not look at me.

"I order you to come back to the car and cut brush," I said. The one sergeant turned. "We have to go on. In a little while you will be cut off. You can't order us. You're not our officer."

"I order you to cut brush," I said. They turned and started down the road.

"Halt," I said. They kept on down the muddy road, the hedge on either side. "I order you to halt," I called. They went a little faster. I opened up my holster, took the pistol, aimed at the one who had talked the most, and fired. I missed and they both started to run. I shot three times and dropped one. The other went through the hedge as he ran across the field. The pistol clicked empty and I put in another clip. I saw it was too far to shoot at the second sergeant. He was far across the field running, his head held low. I commenced to reload the empty clip.[13]

There are not many images here and nothing about the sensations that Frederic Henry felt at the time. He only reports the actions that took place—to shoot first at the talkative sergeant and then to determine that the second one was too far away to be hit. But one must remember the emotional pressures on Frederic Henry at the moment rather than when he tells about it later. First, he has made a decision and followed it with a course of action that now appears to be a mistake. Second, he recognizes that the two sergeants do not trust his judgment and do not accept him and his men ("They hated the lot of us."[14]). He has already reprimanded one of the sergeants for looting, but at least the man followed orders at that time. Finally, they have challenged his authority. Because of these emotional pressures, Frederic Henry acts. He shoots one of the sergeants, "the one who had talked the most."

The man is only wounded, and Bonello—who later will

also lose confidence in Henry's leadership and will desert—asks permission to finish off the sergeant. Lieutenant Henry not only gives him the gun, but tells him how to cock it properly when it misfires the first time.

How important this scene is to the total effect of the novel has not been adequately discussed, although E. M. Halliday has pointed to the irony of the incident as it compares to Frederic Henry's own escape later.

The climax of this grim comedy is of course Frederic Henry's own desertion. Threatened with military justice akin to that he so summarily had dealt the sergeant, he dives into the Tagliamento River; and his sarcastic remarks on his would-be executioners ring with hyperironic overtones against the baffle of the earlier incident. . . .[15]

It is hard to disagree with Halliday that the military justice of the Carabiniere is not distinct from Lieutenant Henry's own justice. Though he had been wounded, he is still not a combat soldier any more than are the Carabiniere. The sergeant might well have argued that in a retreat you do not argue with an officer who is obviously going to get you captured, and that, in particular, you do not obey an officer who is not your own officer, is not a combat officer, and who speaks with an accent. Nor did Lieutenant Henry conduct a trial. He shot first at the one who talked the most and whom he obviously disliked the most, knowing that a dead soldier is no more help at pushing trucks than one who has run away. He has acted quite differently from the way he had acted in helping the soldier who had been to Pittsburgh.

Years after the incident, Frederic Henry as narrator chooses to report it unemotionally. There is little mention of it after the incident is described, except for an admission of guilt. " 'We'll dig out and try once more with the brush,' I said. I looked down the road. It was my fault. I had led them up here. The sun was almost out from behind the clouds and the body of the sergeant lay beside the hedge."[16] His admission of guilt for the loss of the ambulances and for putting his men in their helpless position also includes guilt for the dead sergeant. The man was killed seemingly without emotion but actually because of a combination of spite and frustration, motivations much the same as those that inspire the wholesale killing of officers later by the Carabiniere. Frederic Henry has been responsible for the unnecessary death of a retreating soldier.

When Lieutenant Henry makes his own escape later, he resembles the sergeant who breaks, running through the hedge, "his head low." "I ducked down, pushed between two men, and ran for the river, my head down."[17]

As Halliday points out, Lieutenant Henry changes his perspective when he hears the Carabiniere questioning the officers. Even more important is the fact that, after he has escaped, Frederic Henry denies the responsibility that he has already admitted.

You had lost your cars and your men as a floorwalker loses the stock of his department in a fire. There was, however, no insurance. You were out of it now. You had no more obligation. If they shot floorwalkers after a fire in the department store because they spoke with an accent they had always had, then certainly the floorwalkers would not be expected to return when the store opened again for business.[18]

The analogy is not quite accurate. Lieutenant Henry has already admitted his responsibility, which is more than that of a floorwalker. It is curious here, I think, that the narrator switches to the second person in reporting his thought, perhaps to suggest that this was his thinking at the time, but also almost as though he were attempting to enlist the reader's involvement and sympathy in his own rationalizations.

His own escape was Lieutenant Henry's farewell to military arms. Malcolm Cowley has suggested that his swim in the Tagliamento is symbolic of baptism and rebirth. But a rebirth into what? From the imagery in the first chapter we recognize a rather unusual and ironic use of the water symbol. The soldiers walk in the rain, and rain means death. Catherine sees herself dead in the rain. I think it becomes fairly clear from the rest of the novel that Frederic has been bathed in the waters of death, not life, and that he is reborn, if at all, into death in life.

When he shoots the sergeant, he fails himself. He becomes inhuman. He accepts and acts by a military code that he later becomes unable to accept or act by when it is applied to him. When he deserts, he makes his farewell to military arms. He makes his separate peace, not like the wounded Nick in *in our time* because he thinks he is dying, but by deserting in order to save his life.

Frederic Henry not only makes a farewell to military arms, he also says farewell to the arms of love—and almost at the same time. It should be remembered that Frederic describes his first association with Catherine as playing the "game" of love. In the beginning their relationship was nothing but a game of sex, with all the moves calculated. One afternoon while making out his report, Frederic thinks about how he would like to be with Catherine in Milan. He constructs a daydream in a hotel. The dream includes an elevator and a boy who brings ice that will have to be left outside the door because Frederic and Catherine

would not wear any clothes because it was so hot and the win-
dow open and the swallows flying over the roofs of the houses
and when it was dark afterward and you went to the window
very small bats hunting over the houses and close down over
the trees and we would drink the capri and the door locked
and it hot and only a sheet and the whole night and we would
both love each other all night in the hot night in Milan. That
was how it ought to be. I would eat quickly and go and see
Catherine Barkley.[19]

Instead, he drinks with Rinaldi and the others. When he does go to see Catherine, she is indisposed and he learns not to take her lightly. After he is wounded, and the war is no longer a joke to him, he tells us that he falls in love with Catherine the first time she walks into his room.

After they have stayed together in the hospital and have considered themselves married, he thinks of her as his wife. When he and Piani walk together in the retreat, he feels the desire to talk about wives. He makes an effort then to push his love outward to Catherine as external object. Then comes his escape from the Carabiniere. His narrow escape from the firing squad and the fact that Catherine is not there are too much for him. He turns his whole concern back to himself, to self-preservation and to self-love. In a passage rhythmically similar to those in *To Have and Have Not* and *For Whom the Bell Tolls*, where Hemingway attempts to describe the emotional qualities of sexual intercourse, and in one of the most bizarre Freudian settings in modern literature, Frederic Henry recalls his act of masturbation.

I could remember Catherine but I knew I would get crazy if I thought about her when I was not sure yet I would see her, so I would not think about her, only about her a little, only about her with the car going slowly and clickingly, and some light through the canvas and my lying on the floor of the car. Hard as the floor of the car to lie not thinking only feeling, having been away too long, the clothes wet and the floor moving only a little each time and lonesome inside and alone with wet clothing and floor for a wife.[20]

At this point, Frederic switches to the second person.

You did not love the floor of a flat-car nor guns with canvas jackets and smell of vaselined metal or a canvas that rain leaked through, although it is very fine under a canvas and pleasant with guns; but you loved some one else whom now you knew was not even to be pretended there; you seeing now very clearly and coldly—not so coldly as emptily. You saw emptily, lying on your stomach, having been present when one army moved back and another came forward. You had lost your cars. . . .[21]

This scene in which Frederic remembers giving in to his sexual desire is blended into his rationalization of the loss of his men—emptiness leading into emptiness. At this point in the novel Frederic Henry reports the moment at which he essentially said farewell to the arms of love. It is his own self-involvement, accentuated by his close escape from death, that makes him break the code of love. And once more he shifts to the second person to involve the reader and to keep from revealing too much about himself.

The over-all symbolic structure of the novel makes these two scenes even more important than they appear when taken out of context. A constantly recurring dichotomy exists in *A Farewell to Arms,* much as it did in *The Sun Also Rises,* between reason and emotion, or between objectivity and subjectivity. Many critics have commented on the light and dark or day and night symbolism. The latter is closely allied to the symbolism which results from a contrast of characters as they represent different ways of life and of thinking about life.

Early in the novel Frederic Henry clearly states that he learned something from his war experiences although he did not profit by the knowledge. In reflecting on his conversation with the young priest, Frederic Henry says, "He had always known what I did not know and what, when I learned it, I was always able to forget. But I did not know that then, although I learned it later."[22] What he learned was that the subjective loyalties were the ones of value, and that the objective view of life resulted in an emphasis on what psychologists would call the basic drives, and especially the drives of sex and self-preservation. Although Frederic Henry is able to realize at times the force of love, he is never able, like Catherine, to sacrifice himself for someone else. Thus he is left alone at the end of the novel.

He has failed to be loyal to the subjective vision of life exemplified in the novel by the priest and Catherine; he is dominated by the objective vision he is too weak to dominate.

From the treatment of the officers in the mess and their treatment of the priest, we are made aware of the difference between the subjective and the objective visions of life. The priest is obviously the symbolic representation of the subjective part of experience. He is the one who points out to Frederic that he should have vacationed in the Abruzzi, where girls should not hear the flute at night, where there is good hunting with a sense of morality about it, and where the old order still exists. It is also the place where, as the priest says, "it is understood that a man may love God. It is not a dirty joke."[23] The priest is the one who also tells Frederic about love. "What you tell me about in the nights. That is not love. That is only passion and lust. When you love you wish to do things for. You wish to sacrifice for. You wish to serve."[24] The priest talks to Frederic primarily about sacred love, for he has never loved a woman; but Count Greffi later indicates to Frederic that love—that is, secular love—is also a religious feeling.

The priest and his subjective way of life are the butt of all the jokes at the mess. Although at first Rinaldi is not the leader of the priest-baiters, he is certainly sympathetic with them. He soon joins their activities, encourages them, and finally is the only one left in the original group. For the most part, these officers represent a materialistic view of the world. They have substituted sensual pleasure for spiritual sacrifice, and they refuse to believe in spiritual love. Since they understand only sensual and material pleasures, they accuse the priest and the priesthood of being motivated by the same desires. Their most repeated and most pointed accusation is sexual in nature. In their frequent references to "five against one," they are accusing the priest of masturbation. John Killinger recognizes the reference correctly, but obviously misinterprets when he says, ". . . in Hemingway's world . . . his opinion of even a good priest is 'five-against-one' or spiritual masturbation and infertility . . . and all religions are a 'joke' on all the people who have them."[25]

In the first place, it is not Hemingway's opinion that a good priest is "five-against-one," or spiritual masturbation; it is not even Frederic Henry's opinion, for he is merely reporting the statements made by the officers.[26] These officers see the world materialistically and thus do not understand, as the priest does, that a man might love God. They are the product of a Godless age. Rinaldi, in some ways, is their prophet, or at least their representative. He is a scientist, and his interest in the war is in perfecting his technique as a doctor. As he tells Frederic, "Oh you should see what I did in the removal of three metres of small intestine and better now than ever. It is one for the *Lancet*."[27]

As scientist, Rinaldi represents reason against emotion. He jokes about Catherine Barkley's morals, about Frederic Henry's naivete—which, in a sense, is part moral in nature. He confesses to Frederic that all his life he has encountered sacred objects, but that he holds nothing sacred. He explains how reason has disrupted his friendships after a subjective relationship has been established between people.

"*I haven't [any married friends],*" *Rinaldi said.* "*Not if they love each other.*"

"*Why not?*"

"*They don't like me.*"

"*Why not?*"

"*I am the snake. I am the snake of reason.*"

"*You're getting mixed. The apple was reason.*"

"*No, it was the snake.*"[28]

Rinaldi is right. The iconoclastic nature of scientific reason has destroyed the old values, and there is nothing to replace them. All that Rinaldi has left, he confesses, is his work. There are only two things in life for him; one is liquor, which hurts his work; the other is sex, which is over in fifteen minutes or less and, as he finds out later, can be dangerous.

Frederic Henry is torn between the two poles. Like Jake Barnes in the earlier novel, he tries to make an adjustment, but his physical side, more virile than Jake's, and the chaotic nature of war and its pressures on the individual do not allow him the vision necessary to make the adjustment. Self-preservation and the sexual desire, as the behavioristic psychologists would agree, and as naturalistic novelists frequently demonstrate, are the dominating forces in his life. Early in the novel Frederic Henry comments on the pull of these forces.

That night at the mess I sat next to the priest and he was disappointed and suddenly hurt that I had not gone to the Abruzzi. He had written to his father that I was coming and they had made preparations. I myself felt as badly as he did and could not understand why I had not gone. It was what I had wanted to do and I tried to explain how one thing had led to another and finally he saw it and understood that I had really wanted to go and it was almost all right. I had drunk much wine and afterward coffee and Strega and I explained, winefully, how we did not do the things we wanted to do; we never did such things."[29]

Frederic Henry recognizes what he "wants" to do, but also that this takes a power of will which he does not have. As he suggests, one does not do what one wants to do because one does not direct his own life—"one thing leads to another." This is, of course, consistent with the way the young Frederic acts throughout the novel as the older Frederic narrates it. He is dominated by forces over which he feels he has no control. They shape his life and, finally, they destroy Catherine.

Ironically, the same forces that Frederic Henry is unable to control—the desire for self-preservation and the sexual desire—are the forces which cause Catherine's destruction, but only because she *is* able to control them. A combination of her willingness to become "part of him," and what James Light has called her service to "selflessness,"[30] or love, and her desire to save Henry from a firing squad are responsible for her own death. First, she becomes pregnant through her selflessness ("I want to do what you want to do") and then she leaves her relatively safe position in order to help row Frederic to Switzerland. When she realizes she has fallen in love, she controls the life around her. When Frederic receives his papers for a convalescent leave, she immediately plans to go with him. He thinks it might be hard to manage, but she tells him that she has realized that big obstacles become small now. "If necessary I'll simply leave," she says. Later she overcomes her sense of conventional morality for his sake when they must take a plushly decorated hotel room the night he leaves for the front.

Frederic Henry, on the other hand, is motivated by his own fears and his own desires. He expects too much without offering anything in return. After he learns to love, it is too late and, as he remarks early in the novel, it was always too easy to forget. There is a strong sense of irony in his remark to Catherine when she examines his blistered hands, "There's no hole in my side."[31] Christ's wounds resulted from sacrifice; Frederic's were received trying to preserve himself. Catherine, however, breaks through all the barriers of selfishness that stand in the way of their happiness. She does this even though she has seen herself dead in the rain. *She* is capable of sacrifice. In contrast to Catherine's subjective selflessness, Frederic Henry's materialistic philosophy has not been large enough to allow him to make love into a religion. He is too concerned with remaining alive. When Catherine is dying he thinks about the dead child. "Poor little kid. I wished to hell I'd been choked like that."[32] But he does not convince even himself. "No, I didn't. Still there would not be all this dying to go through." Catherine, however, knows that death is just a "dirty trick."[33]

Frederic Henry's failures and his further inability to accept his responsibilities are, I assume, at the basis of Holden Caulfield's rejection of him as a "phony." But at least Frederic Henry does not make himself out a hero. Nor does Hemingway. John Killinger's estimate of the concluding philosophy of the novel and of Hemingway's handling of the material is inaccurate because he has failed to separate Hemingway from his narrator. Killinger says that

Henry's philippic against the impersonal "they" that kills you—that killed Aymo gratuituously [sic], that gave Rinaldi the syphilis, and that now is killing Catherine—is fine rhetoric and perhaps much in place for a universe without God in our time, but it is the author himself who is guilty of Catherine's death because of his fondness for the hero, and who makes a scapegoat of the world.[34]

Even were it true that the world is made a scapegoat, it is not the author who makes it so; it is Frederic Henry, the narrator. This is a very important distinction, especially if we do not assume with Killinger that Hemingway is fond of his "hero." For, in reality, Frederic Henry is not the hero —Catherine is. Even a cursory view of most of the war novels that preceded *A Farewell to Arms* will show the difference between Frederic Henry and the other central male characters. In almost all of these novels that Hemingway mentions in his introduction to *Men at War,* and all of which we expect him to have read, the heroes are young and brave men who are broken by the war; they are either physically killed, as in Frederic Manning's *Her Privates We,* or they are destroyed spiritually, as in Thomas Boyd's *Through the Wheat.* Always it is the horror of war or the system that is the destructive element. Through the use of the first-person narrator, Hemingway has been able to show the forces of war acting on the individual. Frederic Henry, unlike the heroes of the other novels who are victims only, helps to destroy himself, and helps to destroy Catherine. As narrator, he may well set up a protective device at times, but the reader is able to see through it because of what Hemingway has Lieutenant Henry tell. In the telling he makes it clear that he is not heroic—not one of the brave—but that Catherine is. "If people bring so much courage to this world the world has to kill them, so of course it kills them. The world breaks every one and afterward many are strong at the broken places. But those that will not break it kills. It kills the very good and the very gentle and the very brave. . . ."[35] The world has killed Catherine Barkley. It only breaks Frederic.

Certainly the selection and presentation of material are evidence of Hemingway's awareness of Frederic Henry's guilt. Such an awareness is most obvious in an examination of the scenes in which Frederic shoots the sergeant and masturbates in the flatcar. Most important, too, are the feelings he has about deserting the army. When at the end of the novel he reminisces about that period of time he spent with Catherine in Switzerland, we have the feeling that in retrospect Frederic protests too much about the sense of serenity he felt and the sense of detachment he had from the war. As he tells it he constantly includes details that contradict what he says on the surface. He remembers going to the gymnasium and boxing a bit, growing a beard, watching Catherine get her hair fixed, but on the whole we see him as a rather aimless man trying to find something to do with himself. The peace and calm he mentions, his

ability to sleep at night, the comparison of their relationship with the people with whom they stay are too much.

> We bought books and magazines in the town and a copy of
> "Hoyle" and learned many two-handed card games. The small
> room with the stove was our living-room. There were two com-
> fortable chairs and a table for books and magazines and we
> played cards on the dining-table when it was cleared away. Mr.
> and Mrs. Guttingen lived downstairs and we would hear them
> talking sometimes in the evening and they were very happy
> together too. He had been a headwaiter and she had worked
> as a maid in the same hotel and they had saved their money
> to buy this place. They had a son who was studying to be a
> headwaiter.[36]

Apparently, like the old retired couple, they have settled
down to a passive existence enjoying each other's company
by playing card games. The sense of isolation from the
world while they are in Switzerland is almost suffocating in
its detail. One suspects that Frederic is rationalizing this
experience too, now that Catherine is dead.

The idyllic quality of this part of the novel, then, seems
to be treated much like Frederic's description of how he
felt about the war and about his desertion from it. Usually
the description of how distant he was from it is tempered
by a statement that indicates his interest in it. For example,
he recalls. "The war seemed as far away as the football
games of some one else's college. But I knew from the
papers that they were still fighting in the mountains because the snow would not come."[37] We see it again when
Catherine and Frederic are discussing their happiness.

"*I have a fine time. Don't we have a good life?*" [Frederic]

"*I do, but I thought maybe you were restless.*"

"*No. Sometimes I wonder about the front and about people I know but I don't worry. I don't think about anything much.*"

"*Who do you wonder about?*"

"*About Rinaldi and the priest and lots of people I know. But I don't think about them much. I don't want to think about the war. I'm through with it.*"[38]

He makes the point that he does not think about the war because he does not want to think about it. But it constantly intrudes. With it comes his feeling of guilt. As he tells Catherine before they leave for Switzerland, "I feel like a criminal. I've deserted from the army."[39] He qualifies this statement later by telling her that he does not feel like a criminal when he is with her. But even in Switzerland the war intrudes on their home atmosphere. "I ordered a whiskey and soda and lay on the bed and read the papers I had bought at the station. It was March, 1918, and the German offensive had started in France. I drank the whiskey and soda and read while Catherine unpacked and moved around the room."[40]

Even when Catherine is dying, Frederic cannot escape the war. He goes to a cafe. "I drank several glasses of beer. I was not thinking at all but read the paper of the man opposite me. It was about the breakthrough on the British front."[41]

As Malcolm Cowley has suggested,

There is . . . a symbolic reason for Catherine's death at this moment. When Frederic Henry made his farewell to armies, he became incapable of living in any sort of community, even a community of two: that is, he became incapable of lasting sexual love. Catherine has to die because the hero must henceforth live alone.[42]

Even more to the point, I think, Catherine must die, in terms of the philosophy expressed in the novel, because she is brave and gentle and good. She dies because she is heroic in the face of death and has known what Frederic Henry did not know or forgot or did not know until too late. It is something that the priest has known all along and that the preacher in Ecclesiastes had expressed about the battle of life. "There is no man that hath power over the spirit to retain the spirit; neither hath he power in the day of death: and there is no discharge in that war. . . ." Like the major in "In Another Country," Frederic Henry has lost the one he loved. Ironically, the female dies rather than the male, who was exposed to the dangers of war. Even more effectively handled in the novel, the death occurs in an attempt to bring life into the world after the male is "safe."

Much has been said about the deterministic attitude of Frederic Henry and about Hemingway as the guiding force behind him. In such discussions, frequent reference is made to the long passage in which Frederic uses the metaphor of the ants on a burning log to represent people in a hostile universe.

Once in camp I put a log on top of the fire and it was full of ants. As it commenced to burn, the ants swarmed out and went first toward the centre where the fire was; then turned back and ran toward the end. When there were enough on the

end they fell off into the fire. Some got out, their bodies burnt
and flattened, and went off not knowing where they were
going. But most of them went toward the fire and then back
toward the end and swarmed on the cool end and finally fell
off into the fire. I remember thinking at the time that it was
the end of the world and a splendid chance to be a messiah
and lift the log off the fire and throw it out where the ants
could get off onto the ground. But I did not do anything but
throw a tin cup of water on the log, so that I would have the
cup empty to put whiskey in before I added water to it. I think
the cup of water on the burning logs only steamed the ants.[43]

James Light suggests that the "messiah," or divinity, is selfish in pouring out the water from his cup onto the ants.
The essential point to be derived from the analogy, however, is that, as Frederic sees him, the messiah is not selfish
but completely indifferent. He could move the log, but
he does not. He does not pour the water selfishly, nor with
any hostility. He pours the water out because, as Hemingway certainly knew, you do not add whiskey to water, you
add water to whiskey. That is the natural order of things,
and therefore the cup must be emptied of water so that the
natural order may be followed. And the rain that falls from
the cup only makes things more difficult for the ants, as
rain makes life difficult for the people in the novel.

But it is not just Hemingway's knowledge of mixing
drinks that must determine the meaning of the analogy.
It is Frederic Henry's analogy after all. The reader has
already been made quite aware that Frederic is rather particular about the way he is served. Just a few pages before

there is a scene in which a waiter has inadvertently put ice in the glass.

I went back to the papers and poured the soda slowly over the ice into the whiskey. I would have to tell them not to put ice in the whiskey. Let them bring the ice separately. That way you could tell how much whiskey there was and it would not suddenly be too thin from the soda. I would get a bottle of whiskey and have them bring ice and soda. That was the sensible way.[44]

As in the following passage about death, the importance in the novel is the significance given to the material by the narrator. We see in his attitude toward life and death a sense of bitterness. And we notice that he has once again shifted into the second person to involve the reader.

That was what you did. You died. You did not know what it was about. You never had time to learn. They threw you in and told you the rules and the first time they caught you off base they killed you. Or they killed you gratuitously like Aymo. Or gave you the syphilis like Rinaldi. But they killed you in the end. You could count on that. Stay around and they would kill you.[45]

Here there is no hint of the concept of the continuum that allows *The Sun Also Rises* to achieve a recognition of the earth abiding forever. Nor has Frederic Henry, as did Jake Barnes, been able to arrive at any ironical or satirical view of life which will allow him to view with resignation the tragedies of life and death. Frederic Henry is completely deterministic and is blaming the unidentified forces of the universe, the "they." His reaction is only the bitterness derived from the knowledge that Catherine is dead, a fact of which he is aware, of course, before he begins to tell the story. There is no awareness, no philosophical resignation in the face of death that we find in the original conclusion to the novel, and this is consistent with the character of Frederic Henry; his bitterness strikes out against the world to disguise his own guilt.

Frederic Henry, placing value upon only the materialistic aspects of experience and unable, like Catherine, to will the subjective values into action by giving up his selfish attributes, has been too concerned about "Time's winged chariot" throughout the novel. Through Hemingway's effective handling of focus of narration, we are able to see the guilt of which Lieutenant Henry is consciously unaware, but which conditions his telling of the story. He may make a separate peace with the armies, and he may turn all his concerns to self-preservation, but there is no discharge from the war against death. Any desertion from that contest is only destructive of the ego. Hemingway has often explained that he had recognized his own mortality after he had been wounded in Italy, that he had suffered from fear, but that he had finally recognized that a man can die but once and that how a man lived and faced death was of most importance. Frederic Henry has discovered this as well, and recognizes his own failure. He tells his story with bitterness as he describes the chaotic world in which he and Catherine lived and loved. In the telling, however, he also describes a heroine who sacrifices for love and who faces death as bravely as Maera or any of the bullfighters Hemingway has described.

In the original conclusion the narrator emphasizes his sense of loss by stating what he could tell about during his empty life after Catherine's death. He concludes, "I could tell what has happened since then, but that is the end of the story."[46] By changing the ending, Hemingway has pointed up that the death of the heroine *is* the end of the story and that the narrator has become subordinated to a secondary position. Hemingway is not, as Killinger has suggested, overly fond of the "hero." Frederic Henry is not, in fact, a hero, and it is the irony implicit in Lieutenant Henry's narration—by which Hemingway subtly allows him to expose his own weaknesses—that is largely responsible for the effectiveness of the novel. At least Frederic Henry has learned about death, and that the life that merely "goes on" is no more than existence. In narrating his story, he does not elaborate on his own failures and his own involvement in Catherine's death, but the details are there to be discovered. They are only slightly disguised by his outcries against the unfairness of the world, and they finally become obvious when contrasted with Catherine Barkley's heroism.

IV

TO HAVE
AND
HAVE NOT:

The Self-Destructive Anti-HERO

THERE IS RATHER general agreement among critics that *To Have and Have Not* is Hemingway's least successful novel. It has been referred to as "the most carelessly constructed of his novels,"[1] "the poorest novel he has written,"[2] and "a book which has no more unity than a sandwich."[3] Even Carlos Baker has admitted that "What had looked in theory like a feasible scheme of moral contrast became in practice a novel divided against itself."[4] The recognition that the novel is indeed a failure does not, however, make it any the less interesting for critical analysis, although it does make it more difficult to evaluate. But it is a novel that is particularly important in terms of Hemingway's development of the hero, for it marks his final work in which the anti-hero is the central character.

Sheridan Baker has said that *To Have and Have Not* is Hemingway's first novel "to create a hero."[5] Such a statement needs a good deal of qualification. Hemingway had already created heroes in Romero of *The Sun Also Rises* and Catherine Barkley of *A Farewell to Arms*. In *To Have and Have Not* Hemingway creates a masculine, individualistic, virile character who is the protagonist of the major plot and who theoretically is contrasted with a decadent ineffectual protagonist in the minor plot. The question of whether or not Harry Morgan is actually a hero becomes an extremely important one. Much of the pejorative criticism of *To Have and Have Not* has resulted from a feeling by critics that Hemingway was blind to the unscrupulousness of the protagonist he had created. Other critics have attacked the novel's structure but have protected Harry Morgan as the individualistic hero. For example, Carlos Baker says that:

If one wishes to see it as an instance of "cultural synechdoche," there is no difficulty in taking Morgan as the type of the old self-reliant individualist confronted by an ever-encroaching social restraint—the civil disobedient who, like Thoreau, is opposed in principle to a corrupt federalism, but is unwilling, having never heard of Thoreau's program, to content himself with passive resistance.[6]

It is certainly true that Harry Morgan is an individualist who is resisting social restraint, but he can hardly be called a Thoreauvian. Thoreau insisted that man must act from a moral conscience, that he should not pursue his own course of action "sitting upon another man's shoulders," and that the good man should give himself to his fellow men. This is distinctly not the portrait of Harry Morgan. Harry Morgan is not a hero; he is an anti-hero. Richard Gordon, the protagonist of the lesser story, is an anti-hero too, but of a different sort.

There are no heroes in *To Have and Have Not,* and yet the novel seems obviously structured for a hero, either as the protagonist of the Morgan plot, or the Gordon plot, or in some position in the center by which the action of the two men can be judged. Unfortunately, there is no axis around which the plots may spin. In an effort to find a hero, critics have sometimes seen Morgan's insolence as dignity, his bravado as courage, his stubbornness as purposefulness and finally his self-pity as awareness. In reality the novel gives us a portrait of the fascist mind in both its violent and decadent forms. If we see the novel, as Carlos Baker suggests, as the death of individualism, then we see individualism dying from excesses at both ends, for there are no heroes in the world Hemingway created in *To Have and Have Not.* As Robert Lewis has pointed out:

On the basis of this philosophy of rugged individualism and of the ends justifying the means, all men will perish—the tough Harry Morgans, the deceitful and deceived Richard Gordons, the idealistic yet brutal revolutionaries, and the fraudulent captains of industry. For some the recognition comes late, for some not at all—they only sense their illness and know not its cause. But all their hollow ships will crash on the rocks of loneliness. When a society is characterized and dominated by excessive concern for the isolated individual (the self), the society too will crash and disintegrate.[7]

Certainly there are qualities of the heroic in Harry Morgan, and these are his aggressiveness, animal vitality, virility, and "individualism." All of these qualities might well be part of the heroic character, but they do not automatically make a character a hero. Harry also possesses characteristics which are definitely not heroic, and some of these cause technical problems in the novel. For one, Harry's intelligence is rather limited. Thus, in those parts which he narrates, he is able to describe only his immediate surroundings and those things that have to do with his occupation; he is unable to note other types of detail or to draw inferences from events in the manner of Jake Barnes or Frederic Henry. This not only limits him as a heroic character, but also makes him a limited narrator.

For another, he is suspicious and, as a result, often clever, but even his cleverness causes problems in the novel. For example, in the limited space of Part I, originally published as a story in *Esquire*, he is pictured as the victim of a Mr. Johnson who has skipped back to the mainland without paying his bill. Even in the short space of this part, we do not believe that a man like Harry Morgan would ever have trusted a man like Johnson. As we see his suspicious nature in the rest of the novel, this original incident that supposedly triggers the downfall of Harry Morgan becomes even more incredible. Harry trusts no one else in the novel but is more trusting of Mr. Johnson than the reader would be. Mr. Johnson is obviously disgusted with his whole trip, has put off paying his bill, quibbles over what he is expected to pay, and gets extremely nervous every time money is mentioned. Furthermore, his excuse that he can save time by taking another boat back to the mainland just does not ring true, for he must wait an extra day to catch the boat. The reader has difficulty believing that Harry Morgan would ever have let a fish like Mr. Johnson get away.

Even more important, Harry's vision is limited to his own motivations. He sees everyone through his own selfishly individualistic view of the world. He has no awareness of others and their feelings, as Jake did, nor any feelings of guilt, as Frederic Henry did. He sees nothing complexly. When, for example, he decides that he must kill the rummy Eddie after Eddie has stowed away on a return trip to the mainland, Harry makes the decision without any consideration of alternatives, and there were many. Because he feels superior to Eddie, he is willing to kill him if necessary to protect the boat. He kills Mr. Sing unnecessarily in order, he says, to keep from having to kill the other Chinamen, although a bit of thinking would have made any killing unnecessary. He has no feelings about leaving the Chinamen in Cuba, nor does he feel any moral twinge when he kills Mr. Sing. He has nothing but contempt for Bee-lips, or for the tourists, or for any of those with whom he deals. His treatment of Albert is especially illuminating. He harangues Albert about not making enough money on relief to keep his children from starving and presents the picture of a cruel and tyrannous government that does not reward its workers adequately. Yet Harry is quite vague when Albert asks how much money he will make off the trip with Harry. Albert says,

"I'd just as soon go if there's any money in it."
"Listen," he said. "You're making seven dollars and a half

a week. You got three kids in school that are hungry at noon. You got a family that their bellies hurt and I give you a chance to make a little money."

"You ain't said how much money. You got to have money for taking chances."

"There ain't much money in any kind of chances now, Al," he said.[8]

The reader will remember that the big-hearted Harry had paid Eddie "the same four dollars a day just as if Johnson had paid" for the chances Eddie took. For a short while Harry thinks he will not take Albert along, then changes his mind when he realizes that Albert is necessary to the fulfillment of his plans. But he does not warn Albert of the danger or of any of the realities of the situation. It is only because Albert does not know what to expect that he is killed. Harry thinks, half in pity and half in contempt, "The poor hungry bastard," but he does not once think that he, as much as the revolutionary who pulled the trigger, is responsible for Albert's death.

There are only a few indications that Harry Morgan has feelings for others. The most obvious example is in his relationship with Marie. He treats her with a certain respect and a certain comradeship that is different from the way he treats everyone else. He does tell Frankie not to get into any trouble over him when Frankie volunteers to find him a way to make some money. There is also the "nigger" who is wounded on the trip in which Harry loses his boat. Harry is sympathetic with the wounded man; yet at one point he would hit the Negro to shut him up. The only reason Harry does not is that he has been shot in the arm and is too weak. Harry also shows respect for Captain Willie Adams, who risks his own license by shouting a warning to Harry and then taking a powerful politician out to sea so that Harry will have time to get away. After Captain Willie has given directions, Harry calls back, "Thanks, brother." But Harry Morgan is not truly of the brotherhood, and he would never have taken such a risk for someone else. Harry has been rather accurately described as

an admirable fellow—good in a boat, good in a bed, good in a fix, with no other ambition than to sustain his family and to hold his head up among his fellows. A little ruthless, perhaps, with the morals of Henry Morgan the pirate, or of Joseph Stalin, who is reputed to have been a robber before he became a dictator.[9]

In his most intense moments, Harry reminds us of a modern Captain Ahab, but the monomania that drives him does not challenge the meaning of the universe. Harry is driven by a romantic attachment to the profession of boating and for monetary "success." Unlike Jake Barnes, Harry Morgan has no wish to learn or to understand. He wishes merely to act, and to think that he acts independently of those around him. Nor is he concerned with the laws or for the rights of others. He judges his actions only in terms of what the actions have achieved financially. He is proud that he has a house of his own, and that he is not on relief, and that his family is better off than the families of others who have grown out of a common environment. Harry's pride is not at all based on any feelings for others. He provides a good home, materialistically, for his children, but he does not like them. He shoves them out of the house at every opportunity, and he tells Marie of his disappointment in them. The self-pride he feels is the foundation of his "aloneness."

Like most individualists, Harry Morgan is not as "self-reliant" as he likes to think. At the end of the novel, a combination of self-pity and self-justification leads him to believe that "a man alone" does not have a chance.[10] But he has wanted to be alone. As he is planning the job for the bank-robbing revolutionists, he thinks, "It would be better alone, anything is better alone but I don't think I can handle it alone."[11] In reality, he has seldom operated alone. Early in the novel he has a crew, including Eddie and a Negro who can bait hooks faster than Harry can. When Mr. Johnson flies back to Miami, leaving Harry stranded without any money, a man named Frankie finds a means for solving Harry's financial difficulties. Later, when Harry has been shot and is practically helpless, it is Captain Willie Adams who calls out a plan of action that Harry should have thought of himself. As Harry remarks, "It was foolish to wait. I felt so dizzy and sicklike I lost my judgment."[12] He is dependent on Bee-lips for his final job with the revolutionaries. After his hidden boat is sighted by the Coast Guard and returned to the docks under guard, he must use another boat and rents one from Freddy Wallace. He is not even able to pay the full price to Freddy. Freddy "trusts" him for $320.

At one point in the novel Morgan suggests that he also trusts Freddy. "Listen, I've done business with Freddy since during the war. Twice I've been partners with him and we never had trouble. You know how much stuff I've handled for him. He's the only son-of-a-bitch in this town I *would* trust."[13] But Harry's trust is limited. He trusts Freddy with only a certain amount of information knowing that if he told him how he was actually going to use his boat, Freddy would not rent it. Further, when Freddy says that he will put the money in the safety deposit box at the bank Harry knows will be robbed, Harry does not warn him. Harry looks knowingly at Bee-lips, says "That's a good place," and grins at the joke. Harry has no sense of loyalty. The reader can only borrow Harry's favorite epithet for others and apply it to him. "Some Harry."

In the final analysis, Harry is not alone nor has he ever been. He is a man who chooses to think he is operating alone and who refuses to recognize that he is dependent on others. If he recognized his dependence, he might not be able to use people as he so obviously does. Harry has used the myth of his independence to sit "upon another man's shoulders" in order to establish his own way of life.

Carlos Baker sees Harry Morgan as the "lineal descendant of the American frontiersman, the man who made his own laws and trusted in his own judgments,"[14] and to prove this view he makes a rather sketchy comparison of the environments in which Harry Morgan and Wyatt Earp lived. If Harry Morgan is descended from any type of frontiersman, his lineage would seem to be that of the mountain man. He is reminiscent of someone like Charles "Cannibal Phil" Gardner, who purportedly once ate his companion and another time his Indian wife when he was trapped by winter storms in the mountains.[15]

Harry Morgan is also much like Boone Caudill, the protagonist of A. B. Guthrie's *The Big Sky*. Boone is proud of being a mountain man, just as Harry is proud of being a boatman. In the sense that Boone recognizes that he could never be a farmer or a town-dweller and Harry recognizes that he could never have operated a filling station, both are romantics about their way of life. Neither recognizes the consequences of his own actions. Boone is busily occupied in destroying his own way of life by wiping out the beaver, and Harry Morgan clings to a way of life that is no longer profitable except through jobs that violate the law. They both live violently, killing people they consider inferior; Boone kills Indians and Harry kills Chinamen and Cubans. And neither man will conform to any system of law when it does not allow him to do what he wants. The question that Thoreau would ask of an action would concern its morality. Boone refuses to abide by the laws of his society in the East or the laws of the Indians and finally even breaks the code of the mountain man. For Harry as well, the morality of an action is unimportant.

Harry's lack of morality is pointed up in the satiric chapter of *To Have and Have Not* which Carlos Baker has called an "exemplum" that fails. The chapter fails primarily because it is badly written, but it does present a picture of another "individualist." This man is a sixty-year-old grain broker who is worried because he is being investigated by the Internal Revenue Service. Like Harry, he has through experience gained a "hard, small, tough and lasting insolence, the one permanent thing he had gained and that was truly valid. . . ."[16] Like Harry, he does not think in abstractions but in deals. He possesses extraordinary sexual vitality, like Harry, and has a strong contempt for the suckers. He also feels no remorse about what has happened to the people he has used. The only ways he differs from Harry are in his attitude toward his wife, whom he has used as badly as everyone else, and in the fact that he has a mathematical brain. But the reader, unless he is consciously trying to see Harry Morgan as hero, can hardly fail to see the comparison in the two portraits.

It is in his lack of morality that Harry Morgan fails most as hero. The absence of morality forces both Sheridan Baker and Carlos Baker to go to great lengths in developing a concept of moral character with which to surround Harry Morgan. Sheridan Baker tries to protect Morgan's immoral activities by making him the victim of society and circumstances.

The end is to show Morgan progressively beaten in spite of his splendid intentions and abilities. He is trying to support a wife and three daughters in Key West by chartering his boat for fishing off touristic Havana. Loss of his expensive fishing reel leads to loss of his hire and the end of his fishing. This in turn leads to carrying illegal Chinese, and then to a murder, which ends that possibility. Next he must try the unprofitable rumrunning of the post-Prohibition days. This leads to loss of his arm by gunfire. His crippled arm leads to his arrest, as he tries to bury his treasure of bootlegged liquor in shallow water. This leads to loss of his boat. Determined to make his own living and keep his family off relief, he makes the desperate contract with Cuban revolutionaries that kills him. Everything fits, including a high WPA truck that sights his hidden boat, and the loss of arm that hobbles his shooting.[17]

Marie is far more accurate when she says, "His luck went bad first in Cuba. Then it kept right worse and worse until a Cuban killed him."[18] In the first place, loss of his reel and hire does not lead to the end of his fishing. His bill for Mr. Johnson comes to exactly $925, of which Johnson has already advanced $100. He is paid $1200 by Mr. Sing for carrying the Chinese into another harbor, so that Harry brings home $375 more than he had expected to make. He could have gone back to fishing. The depression had put charter-boat fishing "on the bum," but Captain Willie Adams has a charter. And it is significant that Harry *returns* to rum-running. He has done it before. Even Harry is aware that he could do something else. It is not that he "must" be a rumrunner.

Carlos Baker uses one of John Ruskin's economic definitions to excuse Harry's immorality. He describes this definition as a moral statement in which "having" is seen "as a power whose importance lay 'not only in the quantity or nature of the thing possessed' but also, and more significantly, 'in its suitableness to the person possessing it and in his vital power to use it.'" Then, Baker insists, "Harry Morgan *has* a combination of social courage and personal integrity precisely suited to his character."[19] This is true. He has the courage and integrity of an outlaw and a bully. The statement is not true, however, if we accept the myth of Harry's heroic capabilities. He is not a capable outlaw. Perhaps Harry is his own best critic in this respect, for he often sees his own faults. Sometimes he rationalizes his mistakes, as he does when he is trying to get Albert off the subject of being paid or when he is trying to build up his courage to undertake a dangerous job, but usually he is quite accurate in judging his own failures. When Mr. Johnson gets away, he recognizes, "It was my fault, I should have known better."[20] After he has waited to bring in his boat so that he can save the liquor by hiding it in shallow water, he recognizes that it was foolish to wait.[21] By throwing out the liquor in deep water and hurrying home, he might have saved both the boat and his arm. Finally, he is killed only after he has made another error in judgment by standing up before he is sure that all of the revolutionaries are dead. He does not blame the loss of his arm for any bad shooting; as a matter of fact, his shooting has been very good. He knew the task was almost impossible, and now he thinks, "Who'd have thought I hadn't got him?"[22] Then, as he lies on the floor of the cockpit, he analyzes the situation.

[Marie]'ll get along, I guess. She's a smart woman. I guess we would all have gotten along. I guess it was nuts all right. I guess I bit off much more than I could chew. I shouldn't have tried it. . . . I should have quit trying to go in boats. There's no honest money going in boats any more. . . . Me. Mr. Beelips and Albert. Everybody that had to do with it. These bastards too. It must be an unlucky business. Some unlucky business. I guess what a man like me ought to do is run something like a filling station. Hell, I couldn't run no filling station.[23]

In the last two sentences an important conflict in the Morgan story is made clear. Morgan is a romantic boatman who cannot accept the change when there is no more honest money to be made in boats. They could have "gotten along," but that would not have been suitable for Harry Morgan. He is true to his concept of himself or of what he wants to be, without any real concern about his wife and family. He may have been a capable charter fisherman, but he is not terribly able in that "unlucky business" of the underworld. He probably would not have lasted long as a mountain man either. Philip Young is right when he indicates that "Although Morgan has a very few points of resemblance to the hero, and is usually mistaken for him, he is not really our man."[24]

John Killinger defends Harry by suggesting that his actions are determined by the "cards" he has been dealt, taking an image from Colonel Cantwell of *Across the River and Into the Trees*. He thinks that Harry must carry the revolutionaries and that by doing so he accepts his "situation and reconstitutes the being that is known as Harry Morgan."[25] But there are ways to play the cards according to the rules of the game, and Killinger too overlooks the concept of morality. We could apply the analogy equally well to the central character of the other plot, Richard Gordon. In order to "reconstitute" the being that is Richard Gordon, Gordon should write another bad novel and think that it is great literature and then go find another Helene Bradley.

That Richard Gordon is not a good novelist, that his pretty wife Helen is through with him, and that he is not very capable sexually (while he has an audience) is just about all we know about him. He is the main character of a story that Hemingway told Maxwell Perkins was invented "as a means of throwing Harry Morgan's masculine virtues into bolder relief."[26] It does not actually succeed in doing that unless we are expected to believe that witnesses to the more private moments of his love scenes would not have bothered Harry Morgan. Strangely enough, Harry, not Marie, is the one who worries about waking the girls during the scene in their bedroom. Robert Lewis recognizes that Harry's reservations about sex approach "prudishness."

Nor is the Gordon story convincing as a contrasting illustration of the "haves" of the depression years. But it does serve to show another type of anti-hero, the decadent writer whose selfishness and lack of morality also lead him to doom. Richard Gordon's doom is packed into one day in his life. First he fails sexually with the sophisticated Helene Bradley and gets his face slapped. He returns home to find that his wife is going to leave him for another man. She gives him a lecture about love based on her almost forgotten middle-class moral background. Having just failed at not being enough of a "man of the world" and now finding that he has been too much of one at home, he slaps his wife to get even for being slapped by Helene and decides to spend the evening getting drunk. In his choice of bars he has no more luck than Harry Morgan has in jobs, for he is humiliated even further by discovering how bad his writing is. His evening's drunk resembles a journey into the "dark night" of the soul as he encounters two levels of madness.

He enters the first level of the mad world at the Lilac Time, a bar where he encounters the madness of the economic "haves." The insane Herbert Spellman likes Gordon's novels, but for the wrong reasons. Spellman likes them as an antidote for life. They are for him like opium. He counsels Gordon on madness and tells him that being crazy is like being in love, except that when one is crazy "it always comes out right."

> "I tell you it's the only way to be happy in times like these. What do I care what Douglas Aircraft does. What do I care what A. T. and T. does? They can't touch me. I just pick up one of your books or I take a drink, or I look at Sylvia's [Sidney, the movie star] picture, and I'm happy."[27]

Then he reveals that he is like a lovely little stork. The night before, the proprietor tells Gordon, Spellman thought he was a horse with wings. Finally, Spellman's manager comes to take him away. As he leaves, Spellman warns Gordon not to "let them confuse you."

The next bar in Gordon's journey is peopled by veterans of World War I who have been shunted to the Florida Keys by a desperate government. For one evening Gordon has stepped out of his stereotyped conceptions of the class struggle into the reality of it. The people he sees are human beings at their lowest level. The camaraderie of the veterans is pure animalism, like that of dogs who suddenly stop playing with a bone to tear viciously at each other's throats. Only one man, the Communist organizer, demonstrates any humanity or literacy. As a representative of the class struggle he gives his opinion of Gordon's novels: he calls them "shit." The rest of the veterans fight and maim one another with complete bestiality. It is as though Richard Gordon is Gulliver exposed suddenly to the Yahoos. In their drunken and "happy" innocence, the veterans are oblivious to pain and to their own tragedy. Perhaps their only human attribute is that they think in stereotypes.

Finally, Gordon sees Professor MacWalsey, the man to whom he is losing his wife, and tries to hit him. But the bouncer at Freddy's knocks Gordon out and MacWalsey takes him home in a taxi. Gordon escapes while the professor is getting cigarettes and then staggers homeward, having suffered about as many indignities as is possible in a period of twenty-four hours.

There is, however, another indignity he suffers at the hands of the narrator, for although Harry Morgan is allowed to make a final statement, Richard Gordon is merely commented upon by two other characters. Both of these comments are important to the novel. The first is that made by MacWalsey as he watches Gordon lurching toward home. It is almost the first touch of compassion to be found in the novel.

He watched Richard Gordon lurching down the street until he was out of sight in the shadow from the big trees whose branches dipped down to grow into the ground like roots. What he was thinking as he watched him, was not pleasant. It is a mortal sin, he thought, a grave and deadly sin and a great cruelty, and while technically one's religion may permit the ultimate result, I cannot pardon myself. On the other hand, a surgeon cannot desist while operating for fear of hurting the patient. But why must all the operations in life be performed without an anaesthetic?[28]

The long passage ends with his thinking that "I wish I could help that poor man whom I am wronging." The humility evident in MacWalsey's thoughts contrasts strongly with the pride of Harry Morgan and the selfish irresponsibility of Richard Gordon. But this does not stop Mac-Walsey from taking Gordon's wife; at least he is aware that in saving the woman he is injuring the man. And he is sorry for it. He also recognizes that all of the operations in life are painful, which is much like the statement by Frederic Henry in *A Farewell to Arms* about the ants on a burning log. In this respect it is interesting to note that the opening sentence of MacWalsey's thoughts includes the symbol of the process of life, from dust to dust (or earth to earth) as the trees grow upward and then arch over until the branches grow back into the ground as roots.

The other commentary on Richard Gordon is a vignette. Marie sees him from the car on the way home from Harry's deathbed.

> As they turned onto the worn white coral of the Rocky Road the headlight of the car showed a man walking unsteadily along ahead of them.
>
> "Some poor rummy," thought Marie. "Some poor goddamned rummy."
>
> They passed the man, who had blood on his face, and who kept on unsteadily in the dark after the lights of the car had gone on up the street. It was Richard Gordon on his way home.[29]

This scene is important in two ways. First, as a contrast to a previous scene in which Richard Gordon had seen Marie walking toward home, it emphasizes Gordon's lack of perception as artist and his selfish use of human beings. When Gordon first sees Marie, he constructs an imaginary life for her, a life which shows how wrong his artistic perceptions are, just as he is later shown to be obviously wrong in his stereotyped view of the class struggles. His failure is one of sensibility. He has acquired a few clichés about writing, such as that the artist cannot be limited to bourgeois standards and that he must experience "life." When he sees life walking along, he constructs a stereotyped Freudian interpretation of Marie as the slovenly, frigid, middle-aged housewife whose husband has long since lost interest in her. Then he hurries home to put it on paper. It is also important that besides being wrong about her, his real concern is that he can *use* this person fictionally. Marie is nothing to him but a potential character for his work.[30]

In direct contrast is Marie's view: she thinks Gordon is a rummy. He is not quite that, and we recognize that she has misinterpreted too. But there is nothing in her reaction to her vision of Richard Gordon which she wishes to *use*. Her reaction is one of compassion. Early in the novel Marie says, when watching Eddie leave the house,

> "Poor goddamned rummies," . . . "I pity a rummy."
> "He's a lucky rummy."
> "There ain't no lucky rummies," Marie said. "You know that, Harry."[31]

The commentaries on Gordon by MacWalsey and Marie bring to the end of the novel a new emphasis, one that is evident also in Harry's last speech and in the final chapter in Marie's eulogy of her husband. The emphasis is upon humility as well as compassion for those who must suffer the operations of life without anaesthesia—which means everyone. The world in which the anti-heroes have lived is a world of violence and moral decay. Neither man has had the vision to recognize and preserve the one thing that could have been meaningful enough to make that life bearable. Harry Morgan is too proud; Richard Gordon too vain, if his wife's description of his attitude toward love is accurate.

Early reviewers may have seen *To Have and Have Not* as a social statement from Ernest Hemingway, but the socioeconomic scene is of minor importance. The novel is about people living in the world, as in all of Hemingway's novels, and in this one there is a contrast between an unsatisfactory individualistic and selfish world and an equally unsatisfactory decadent world. Neither world is satisfactory, nor are there any characters in the world who can impose any meaning on it. The ants are still trying to get off the burning log, and the messiah still withholds his hand from giving any relief. He merely pours on more water, increasing the steam in this fictional creation of a horrible and chaotic world.

MacWalsey recognizes the state of things and is resigned to it. He suffers, but the one who suffers most is Marie, who is steamed more than anyone else because she has "had" so much. In the last chapter Marie is presented distinctly and humanly. Her prejudices show through in her hatred for Cubans and Negroes, especially when she remembers how

Harry had humiliated a Negro who had "said something to her." She remembers the strength of their sexual relations, and she remembers that she had nothing to worry about in life with her husband. It is not that her feelings are not also for herself; they are. Nor is it that she pictures Harry as heroic; she does not. She sees him as part of herself that is gone, and her sense of loss does more than anything else in the novel to make the reader feel the impact of Harry's death. As Robert Lewis suggests, "Harry's symbolic goodness in the art of eros was something, at least, and Marie valued it in itself and for what it signified."[32] Her final monologue does most, on reflection, to raise the stature of Harry Morgan. His ability to affect another life other than his own through a love that he has treated with an integrity that he has failed to apply in his relations with others is the quality that is, after all, his most human. In this sense he has not been a man alone, although he has failed to recognize it.

Unfortunately, the book is badly done. It is poorly organized, and the Gordon story is neither an effective contrast to the Morgan story nor a satisfactorily developed parallel story of disintegration through decadence. The work is further confused by shifts in narrative techniques; as E. M. Halliday says, "no positive justification can be found for the display of variety."[33] Technically, Hemingway's use of a variety of narrative perspectives is the most glaring failure of the novel.

Part I is told from the first-person narrative perspective. Harry Morgan tells his own story and, as has already been discussed, Harry Morgan is extremely limited as a narrator.

The narrative perspective of Part I is third-person narration. For most of this section the narrative perspective is centered on the central character, Harry, but soon after the beginning of the second chapter, the narrator shifts his concentration to the action aboard the charter boat *South Florida,* where Captain Willie Adams manages to keep the federal government "alphabet man" Frederick Harrison from identifying Morgan and making an arrest. The third and last chapter of Part II returns to Harry Morgan.

Part III is a hodge-podge of experimentation. The first chapter is first person narration, with the narrator appropriately identified for the reader—*"Albert Speaking."* Here, the reader is presented with a view of Harry Morgan from another perspective. Albert Tracy tells about the incident in which he is hired to go on the trip to Cuba, the trip that will eventually end in his death. Albert is none too sensitive as an interpreter of character, either. He is, for example, only half right when he says that Harry "was mean talking now, all right, and since he was a boy he never had no pity for nobody. But he never had no pity for himself either."[34] He sums up his reactions to Harry in one sentence: "He was a bully and he was bad spoken but I always liked him all right."

The next chapter heading identifies "Harry" as the speaker of a very short first-person monologue. Chapter Eleven, however, begins with a short passage of what appears to be first-person narration from Albert, or at least someone who uses approximately the same level of language Albert has used. "You could see they had given him plenty out at Richard's because when he drinks it makes him cocky and he came in plenty cocky."[35] Only sixteen lines are written from this perspective, mostly a dialogue between Harry, Freddy, and Bee-lips. After a break in type, the chapter continues with an objective third-person narrator following Harry and Bee-lips into one of the back booths. The rest of this short section consists of a dialogue between Harry and Bee-lips. Once more, a break in typography indicates a change of scene, and the final part of the chapter is introduced by a third-person narrator who is not quite so objective. He feels free to interpret the action; for example, "It was as simple as Harry had figured it."[36]

Chapter Thirteen offers a further example of confused narration. The chapter opens with the narrator's description of the scene.

> At ten o'clock in the morning in Freddy's place Harry was standing in against the bar with four or five others, and two customs men had just left. They had asked him about the boat and he had said he did not know anything about it.[37]

After a two-page dialogue between some characters and Harry in Freddy's place, the narrator once more enters. From his diction and attitude, however, he seems to be a different narrator—one of the people at the bar.

> [Hayzooz] goes out with the stranger and the bottle of Bacardi and the laugh is on Rodger all right. That Hayzooz is a character all right. Him and that other Cuban, Sweet-water.[38]

Whoever is doing the narrating, it is not Harry. It is not Albert, for he enters the scene later, and it is obviously not Freddy. Whoever it is, he disappears later in the conversation as Harry and Bee-lips secretly revise their plans because Harry's boat has been discovered.

One other type of narrative perspective is used in Chapter Twenty-four, the satiric chapter describing the people on the boats in the harbor as Harry's body is being brought in. This narrator philosophizes and interprets, and appears to be a remnant of Hemingway's narrative aproach in *Death in the Afternoon* and *Green Hills of Africa*. The narrator comments on the rich as he explains the life of Henry Carpenter:

> If he had not been felt to be cracking up, with that instinct for feeling something wrong with a member of the pack and healthy desire to turn him out, if it is impossible to destroy him, which characterizes the rich; he would not have been reduced to accepting the hospitality of Wallace Johnston.[39]

He also has some commentary on the sexual prowess of college men.

> The fiancé is a Skull and Bones man, voted most likely to succeed, voted most popular, who still thinks more of others than of himself and would be too good for any one except a lovely girl like Frances. He is probably a little too good for Frances too, but it will be years before Frances realizes this, perhaps; and she may never realize it, with luck. The type of man who is tapped for Bones is rarely also tapped for bed; but with a

lovely girl like Frances intention counts as much as perform-
ance.[40]

Only one section of this satiric chapter is effectively narrated, the picture of the narcissistic Dorothy Hollis. In this
final scene of the chapter, the narrator moves from an external description of Mrs. Hollis into her mind. The result
is a striking contrast to Marie's final monologue. Both
women have strong sexual motivations, but Marie's is directly toward Harry. When he is gone, she can think only
of her loss. Mrs. Hollis, on the other hand, finds solace and
satisfaction in herself; "I'm here, I'm always here and I'm
the one that cannot go away, no, never. You sweet one. You
lovely. Yes you are. You lovely, lovely, lovely. Oh, yes,
lovely. And you're me."[41]

Some rather sophomoric philosophizing in this chapter
and an artistically indefensible shifting of narrative perspective in many other chapters reveal a basic weakness in
the storytelling. Both Carlos Baker and Sheridan Baker
have noted that there is a great deal of good writing in the
novel, and some of Hemingway's worst. It becomes obvious
that Hemingway had tried to expand into a novel the short
stories he had published separately in *Cosmopolitan* and
Esquire, neither of which was very significant, and that he
did not take the time to develop the work properly or to
solve the technical problems involved.

The frustration of the many critics who have a great
respect for Hemingway as writer is obvious in their criticism of this novel. Sheridan Baker's recent book furnishes a
good example. He begins by saying that Scribner's published Hemingway's still unsatisfactory novel, but that

"Even so, *To Have and Have Not* comes near to equaling Hemingway's best." When, in his analysis, Baker arrives at Harry Morgan's dying words, however, he is disappointed.

> But Morgan's dying words do not fit. Probable enough, moving enough, Morgan's death nevertheless gives us a message when we want a man. Instead of "a man alone has no chance," we want the uselessness of Morgan's single-handed and single-minded integrity to iluminate its glory. We want another little bullfighter, in another sorry contest, beaten but undefeated.[42]

What Sheridan Baker wants is a novel in which Harry Morgan is the hero. He wants a different novel, for Harry is not a hero. He does not, for example, die like Maera fighting against death to the very last. For Harry Morgan, the pain becomes too much. Marie says, "But finally he was just too tired." Even his dying message indicates his tendency to rationalize. His statements are not only probable enough, they are consistent with what Harry Morgan, as we see him in the novel, would have said. His first words are, "Ain't got no hasn't got any can't really isn't any way out." This perhaps would have made a fitting final statement by itself. But he continues. His next important statement is an analogy. "Like trying to pass cars on the top of hills. On that road in Cuba. On any road. Anywhere. Just like that. I mean how things are. The way that they been going. For a while yes sure all right. Maybe with luck. A man."[43] Here is a picture of a changed world. It is more difficult to live in because there might be a car approaching the crest of the hill from the other side. He recognizes the danger here, but he is obviously not concerned about killing the people in the other car. He is only concerned about whether or not the passing car can make it back into the lane without the driver getting killed. He is not concerned that the laws against passing are designed to protect the occupants of all the cars involved. He is completely in character, of course. Finally he states that "One man alone ain't got. No man alone now. No matter how a man alone ain't got no bloody fucking chance." And this statement contains all the bitterness and hostility and self-pity and self-justification and insolence of the dying anti-hero. Harry dies as an anti-hero just as he has lived as one. Hemingway has at least been true to his characterization. Only after Harry's last words does the narrator slip. "It had taken him a long time to get it out and it had taken him all of his life to learn it," he tells us. But Harry had really become aware of it only after the revolutionary shot him, and becomes aware only because he has been shot.

In one of the few effective images in the novel, Harry's failure is made clear, although Harry is not consciously aware of the meaning. He lies dying with his knees drawn up in almost foetal position and feels

The water of the lake that was his belly was very cold; so cold that when he stepped into its edge it numbed him, and he was extremely cold now and everything tasted of gasoline as though he had been sucking on a hose to syphon a tank. He knew there was no tank although he could feel a cold rubber hose that seemed to have entered his mouth and now was coiled, big, cold, and heavy all down through him. Each time he took

a breath the hose coiled colder and firmer in his lower abdo-
men and he could feel it like a big, smooth-moving snake in
there, above the sloshing of the lake. He was afraid of it, but
although it was in him, it seemed a vast distance away and
what he minded, now, was the cold.[44]

C. G. Jung, in discussing the snake as a symbolic representation of the introverted libido, gives a number of examples of dreams in which the snake coils within the individual.[45] Although Jung suggests that introversion may
cause fertilization, inspiration, regeneration and rebirth,
the symbol used by Hemingway causes Harry to be afraid.
The dominant quality of the coiled hose or snake is its
coldness or sterility. Harry's introverted life force is destructive rather than regenerative. The impossibility of his attempt to face the world alone is demonstrated symbolically
in the paragraph which follows in Harry's attempt to bring
back the warmth of life through pulling the self around
himself.

For a time he had thought that if he could pull himself up
over himself it would warm like a blanket, and he thought for
a while that he had gotten himself pulled up and he had
started to warm. But that warmth was really only the hemor-
rhage produced by raising his knees up; and as the warmth
faded he knew now that you could not pull yourself up over
yourself and there was nothing to do about the cold but take
it.[46]

This is Harry's unconscious awareness of the inability of
man alone to have a chance, and it comes only while he is
dying. He tries to rationalize his actions in talking to the

captain and the mate of the Coast Guard cutter, but finally he must come back to the "man alone."

We know that Harry has not taken his whole life to learn it because before he is shot and while he is thinking that he has successfully killed all four revolutionaries, the narrator tells us that he is already beginning to get a singing, happy feeling. Had he escaped, we can imagine Harry preparing for another adventure and telling another unsuspecting helper, "Me. I ain't gonna let my kids starve but nobody's paying anything for taking chances these days." Then he would use other people in his planning and think that he was doing it all alone. We know that Harry did not learn about a man alone until he was alone with death. We have seen him throughout the novel, and he has not been alone, although he has chosen to believe he was. Harry Morgan is one of the most convincing anti-heroes Hemingway created.

But Harry is placed in the position that would ordinarily be held by a hero, and there seems to be a vacuum without one. There is no one in the novel of enough importance to fill the emptiness.[47] MacWalsey's humility is there, but he is not an important character. Helen Gordon espouses middle-class morality, but in such a sudden emotionalized outburst that the values are sentimentalized. Marie's final statement reflects upon the novel to some extent to enlarge the concept of the man Harry Morgan, but Marie has been too much of a minor character until the last.

Harry's limitations as man and narrator have been too great. He has told only of himself and the practical matters of his unlucky businesses. There has thus been no important symbolism to deepen and enforce the thematic content, as in *The Sun Also Rises* and *A Farewell to Arms*. Nor does the omniscient author provide this enrichment with any consistency. The last image, in which a camera technique is used, is an example. After Marie's monologue, the narrator moves outside the house on a lovely cool day with laughing tourists riding by on bicycles, and a peacock squawks across the street. Then the view moves out to the sea, with a white yacht coming in to harbor and a tanker, seven miles out "hugging the reef as she made to the westward to keep from wasting fuel against the stream."

The Gulf stream has figured largely in the novel, and in one scene it provides the background for a successfully symbolic passage. The dead men and Harry are in the boat, and the fish are eating the blood as it drips into the water. Smoke from a tanker is off in the distance. The scene might suggest the continuum of nature, or especially in this novel, the concept of "nature red in tooth and claw," or an ironic contrast between man's violence and the comparative calm of nature, or the insignificance of all the violence of man in the tiny boat now becalmed in the hugeness of the sea. But there is not enough use of effective symbol, either in this scene or in the novel's final image. One has the tendency, with Sheridan Baker, to "want" something more—something, perhaps, like the symbol of the leopard on the mountain in "The Snows of Kilimanjaro," or the rain in *A Farewell to Arms,* or the bullfight rituals of *The Sun Also Rises.*

But that something more is not in this novel. We can attempt to see the steamer as saving its virility by keeping out of the mainstream of life as suggestive of the safer way that Harry Morgan might have taken. But that does not fit. The image is more appropriately like the original conclusion of *A Farewell to Arms* in which Frederic talks about part of the world stopping and the rest going on, or the conclusion of *The Old Man and the Sea* where the tourists, ironically, are unaware of Santiago's heroism. But the image needs the death of a hero for contrast. In Auden's "Musée des Beaux Arts" it is not the death of a plowman that creates the irony, it is the boy "falling out of the sky." Harry Morgan does not provide us with the martyrdom that must run its course in some untidy spot to create the irony. The image of the world going on may be significant to Marie, but for the reader of the novel it is just a pretty picture.

At best there is some fine writing in this badly confused novel, and Harry Morgan is a convincing anti-hero. He is the last anti-hero as protagonist that Hemingway creates, for with *For Whom the Bell Tolls* he begins to work with the heroic character. *To Have and Have Not* is a novel that might have been successful had Hemingway taken the necessary time with it. But as it was printed, it is a failure despite the tendency of critics to extol its virtues in a reconstruction of what might have been.

V

FOR WHOM
THE BELL
TOLLS:

The Mythic HERO in the Contemporary
world

ONLY THREE YEARS PASSED between the publication of
To Have and Have Not and *For Whom the Bell Tolls*; yet
between the two books great changes had taken place in
Hemingway's approach to the novel and to experience. *For
Whom the Bell Tolls* is written entirely from the omniscient author narrative perspective, it is an essentially romantic novel, and for the first time the male protagonist
is a fully developed hero. These three changes are inextric-
ably involved with one another. They were necessary for an
exploration into a subjective world to which Hemingway
had alluded in both *The Sun Also Rises* and *A Farewell to
Arms,* but which he had not been able to explore in either.

The first-person narrative perspective did not provide an expansive enough technique to deal with it, his naturalistic approach did not offer the required philosophical orientation, and his concentration on the anti-hero and his conception of man at the mercy of a hostile universe gave little possibility for the development of heroic action. Hemingway's change in technique and thinking, however, led to the creation of a hero who is both mythic and modern in concept.

Joseph Campbell has explained the function of the modern hero in his discussion of the contemporary problem.

> *The problem of mankind today . . . is precisely the opposite to that of men in the comparatively stable periods of those great co-ordinating mythologies which now are known as lies. Then all meaning was in the group, in the great anonymous forms, none in the self-expressive individual; today no meaning is in the group—none in the world: all is in the individual. But there the meaning is absolutely unconscious. One does not know toward what one moves. One does not know by what one is propelled. The lines of communication between the conscious and the unconscious zones of the human psyche have all been cut, and we have been split in two.*
>
> *The hero-deed to be wrought is not today what it was in the century of Galileo. Where then there was darkness, now there is light; but also, where light was, there now is darkness. The modern hero-deed must be that of questing to bring to light again the lost Atlantis of the co-ordinated soul.*[1]

The bringing together of the separated aspects of the human soul is exactly the function of Jordan's role in *For Whom the Bell Tolls.* Hemingway has moved from a novel which is a condemnation of individualism to a novel which relates individualism to the group, and has created Robert Jordan as the protagonist who follows the mythical journey of the hero in a modern setting.

Such a task, however, required a different approach to the technical problems of the novel. Hemingway's new omniscient narrative perspective in *For Whom the Bell Tolls* allowed him greater freedom in developing minor characters, in structuring a more complicated story and, finally and most importantly, in presenting a more subjective view of Robert Jordan's world.

By moving into the minds of other characters, the omniscient author could develop in detail characters like Pilar, Pablo, and Anselmo, who thus become concrete and believable members of a group. It is not just what they say and do that is reported to us by the central character, as in *The Sun Also Rises* and *A Farewell to Arms,* but there is also an examination of how they think and feel.

Nor is the story limited only to the activities that a first-person narrator could have witnessed or received second-hand. Through the omniscient author's ability to shift scenes, we are able to relate the microcosmic struggle at the blowing up of the bridge to its macrocosmic extensions beyond the mountains. The use of the omniscient author enables Hemingway to universalize the action through the suspension of time, as Earl Rovit describes,[2] and, most important of all, to allow the reader to see the total world of Robert Jordan. We are not limited to the description and interpretation of action by a first-person narrator frequently concerned with his own problems and restricted to his own personal vision. The narrator of *For Whom the Bell Tolls* is obviously complex; he is very much aware of Jordan's reactions both to the external world and to the world within, and he is able to report both worlds.

Carlos Baker has examined closely the change in Hemingway's artistic technique in *For Whom the Bell Tolls*, and he describes as *ingestion* one aspect of that change made possible by Hemingway's use of the omniscient author.

Without, for example, sacrificing the value of suggestion (where the reader is required to supply his own imaginative clothing for an idea nakedly projected), Hemingway has come round to an appreciation of the value of ingestion. This signifies a bearing within, a willingness to put in, and to allow to operate within the substance of a piece of writing, much that formerly would have been excluded in favor of suggestion.[3]

Certainly this is an accurate description of differences in method, and it is true that in *For Whom the Bell Tolls* Hemingway has "put in" more than he had previously, and that he is "bearing within" the material more than in his naturalistically oriented novels. What it does not explain, however, is that the material included is also suggestive in another sense. The more material presented, the more associations that may be called forth and the "deeper" the associations may go.

In *Death in the Afternoon* Hemingway had written that:

If a writer of prose knows enough about what he is writing about he may omit things that he knows and the reader, if the writer is writing truly enough, will have a feeling of those *things as strongly as though the writer had stated them. The dignity of an ice-berg is due to only one-eighth of it being above water.*[4]

The iceberg is the basic analogy from which Carlos Baker is working in his discussion of ingestion and suggestion. Hemingway's description explains the suggestive principle. The iceberg, however, adequately represents both principles. The larger the visible part of the iceberg, the more there is beneath the surface. Or at least there is always the possibility that there will be more if the writer is writing "truly enough" and is including the type of material that the reader can "feel." In their discussion of William Faulkner, Hoffman and Vickery have explained this phenomenon.

Through his intuition and full use of tone, the artist can sometimes succeed, not in translating but simply in making the individual reader feel the terrible complexity of the world, charged with myths and signs and broken into fragments, in its past, present and future.[5]

This is an accurate description of what Hemingway has achieved through the creation of his own mythology, or what Rovit has called a "fable." The modern adventure of Robert Jordan is archetypal in that it springs from the myths and signs that the subjective passages suggest and that we unconsciously associate with the material. Consequently, the hidden part of the iceberg looms larger and larger and the terrible complexity of the world can be felt beneath the surface of the action.

E. M. Halliday asks, "Does not the preponderance of

subjective passages in *For Whom the Bell Tolls*, by the shift in emphasis away from the solid specifications of the outside world, make that novel less eminently realistic than Hemingway's first two books?"[6] The answer, of course, is affirmative. What becomes apparent is that this is Hemingway's first romantic novel, both in technique and conception. The impetus for his earlier novels may well have been derived from romantic ideas, as Rovit suggests, but his technique was basically naturalistic. This is not so in *For Whom the Bell Tolls*. With this Spanish Civil War novel, Hemingway has become a romantic.

Early criticism of *For Whom the Bell Tolls* was frequently so concerned with the political views of the novel that it did not concern itself with philosophical views. Malcolm Cowley's introduction to *The Portable Hemingway* was among the first essays to describe Hemingway's romantic tendencies.[7] The publication of *The Old Man and the Sea* left little doubt of Hemingway's romanticism, and there is general agreement among critics that the romantic impetus had always been in Hemingway's fiction. Carlos Baker discusses Hemingway's Wordsworthian romanticism in his chapters on *For Whom the Bell Tolls,* but perhaps the most convincing argument for placing Hemingway in the American romantic tradition, linked more closely with Emerson and Whitman than with Hawthorne and Melville, is made by Earl Rovit. There has also been an attempt to classify Hemingway as an existentialist. It seems to me, however, that Hemingway is not really of this school, and the reasons he is not are important to an analysis of *For Whom the Bell Tolls*.

Very generally speaking, the romantic position attempts to bring the diversity of experience into a fundamental, meaningful and harmonious unity. The existentialist, on the other hand, sees that the apparent unity is superficial and discovers greater and more horrible diversity behind the mask. Sartre's hero in *Nausea*, for example, pauses in a park and looks at a tree. He sees the individual leaves and branches finally converging into the trunk of a tree. But then he imagines what is beneath the earth.

And then all of a sudden, there it was, clear as day: existence had suddenly unveiled itself. It had lost the harmless look of an abstract category: it was the very paste of things, this root was kneaded into existence. Or rather, the root, the park gates, the bench, the sparse grass, all that had vanished: the diversity of things, their individuality, were only an appearance, a veneer. This veneer had melted, leaving soft, monstrous masses, all in disorder—naked, in a frightful obscene nakedness.[8]

Thus he finds that the original unity he had seen was superficial because it seemed to indicate meaningfulness. Beneath the surface were the disordered "monstrous masses" which are chaotic and incomprehensible. Faced with that meaninglessness, the existential hero suffers a sense of nausea or despair. Finally, however, through an act of will, he decides to act in the world despite the fact that he knows his actions are useless and meaningless. But if we look at Robert Jordan as a hero, we find that the changes in him do not follow the existential pattern. He does not feel despair or experience nausea in perceiving the discreteness of experience. John Killinger calls attention to Pilar's description of the smell of death as an instance of a description

> not very different from the feeling of dread or nausea belonging to the man who in Heidegger's philosophy runs forward to death, who in Sartre stands poised on the brink of a cliff, and who in Jaspers has travelled much within himself and has discovered death to be one of his boundaries.[9]

The reader may feel nauseous after reading Pilar's description, but one must note that Jordan does *not*, either after the description or anywhere else in the novel. He has disappointments, it is true, but he consistently acts as though he were heeding Bill Gorton's advice to Jake Barnes in *The Sun Also Rises,* "Never be daunted." Robert Jordan's heroic journey throughout the novel is primarily concerned with bringing together the diversity of experience—both subjective and objective—into a meaningful relationship. Thus the journey he undertakes closely resembles the journeys of mythical heroes, not existential heroes.

The mythic-heroic deed which Robert Jordan is to perform follows a generalized and basic plan, although individual variations may occur. In Joseph Campbell's description:

> The mythological hero, setting forth from his commonday hut or castle, is lured, carried away, or else voluntarily proceeds, to the threshold of adventure. There he encounters a shadow presence that guards the passage. The hero may defeat or conciliate this power and go alive into the kingdom of the dark (brother-battle, dragon-battle; offering, charm) or be slain by the opponent and descend in death (dismemberment,

crucifixion). Beyond the threshold, then, the hero journeys through a world of unfamiliar yet strangely intimate forces, some of which severely threaten him (tests), some of which give magical aid (helpers). When he arrives at the nadir of the mythological round, he undergoes a supreme ordeal and gains his reward. The triumph may be represented as the hero's sexual union with the goddess-mother of the world (sacred marriage), his recognition by the father-creator (father atonement), his own divinization (apotheosis), or again—if the powers have remained unfriendly to him—his theft of the boon he came to gain (bride-theft, fire-theft); intrinsically it is an expansion of consciousness and therewith of being (illumination, transfiguration, freedom). The final work is that of the return. If the powers have blessed the hero, he now sets forth under their protection (emissary); if not, he flees and is pursued (transformation, flight, obstacle flight). At the return threshold the transcendental powers must remain behind; the hero emerges from the kingdom of dread (return, resurrection). The boon that he brings restores the world (elixir).[10]

Jordan's blowing up the bridge has both mythical values and a mythical basis, although, because it is a contemporary myth, it does not correspond exactly to the journeys of any popular or literary hero. One of the most important considerations in Robert Jordan's heroic journey is that it is a double one. The more obvious journey is at the physical level and is centered around the task of blowing up a bridge at a precise time through the coordinated action of an individual and a group. The less obvious journey is the moral or spiritual one, for it involves a journey within the hero, a descent into his own unconscious, and the trial involved in bringing that unconscious life into relation with the conscious life. As an exemplum, Robert Jordan's journey must also have meaning for the world at large, and must deal with man's contemporary problem—the "split" between the conscious and the unconscious, in Campbell's description, or, as Erich Fromm describes it: "In the nineteenth century the problem was that *God is Dead*; in the twentieth century the problem is that *man is dead*."[11] Perhaps the most obvious example of Hemingway's own recognition of the problem (other than in the remarkable story "A Clean Well-Lighted Place") is in his refusal to depict a hero in his previous novel. Even Harry Morgan's few heroic qualities become faults because he is isolated from mankind. But Robert Jordan is not isolated, and the two concurrent journeys in which he brings the conscious and the unconscious into a meaningful relation also bring him to a full acceptance of and a total involvement with mankind. He does, in a sense, through his own sacrifice, restore man to life.

His physical or "conscious" journey is rather easily seen. Robert Jordan is asked to volunteer for a mission beyond the lines. The nature of the mission is so extraordinary and dangerous that General Golz cannot "order" him to do it. But Jordan accepts the assignment. He is taken by the guide Anselmo to the threshold of adventure. He is challenged by Pablo, not just at the threshold but throughout the adventure. The tests are all concerned with his ability to achieve the final goal, which is blowing up the bridge. The difficulty is that the bridge must be blown at a precise time. A minor goal in this journey is his sexual union with Maria. In the achievement of both goals he is aided by Pilar, who seems to have almost magical powers. She sends Maria to his sleeping bag, and she usurps Pablo's power when, through his self-interest, he loses the confidence of the group and allows the group to disintegrate. Pablo's treachery complicates Jordan's task even more, as do natural forces in the form of weather, and these complications become further tests of Jordan's capabilities as hero. As he meets them one by one, he is finally able to accomplish the "theft," the blowing of the enemy's bridge. He flees with his group, but at the return threshold, he is denied entrance into the world. As in Christian versions of the myth, he must die, leaving only his influence with his disciples. The fact that the heroic deed does not change the shape of the world is insignificant since the battle need not necessarily be won by the hero. His own action has been a victory and serves primarily as an example to others. In effect, it reunites the group. On the physical level, then, or on the level of the conscious world, the cycle of the hero's adventures has been completed.

But there is an even more important cycle to be discovered. This cycle has to do with the unconscious and, to be effective, must be closely related to the other cycle. What happens in this adventure is a journey into the soul and, in another sense, outward to the subjective areas of experience. It is a journey that no previous Hemingway protagonist has undertaken in a novel. Both Frederic Henry and Jake Barnes had been aware of the existence of an area of experience that they could not understand. They were willing to talk about it in terms of the difference between the night and day, but they had never attempted an exploration of it. Robert Jordan does.

About the structure of the novel, Earl Rovit remarks:

As many critics have pointed out, the structure of For Whom the Bell Tolls is circular; its center, which we are never allowed to be unaware of, is the steel bridge which spans the gorge "in solid-flung metal grace." From that center all the actions of the novel, dramatic and symbolic, radiate in widening concentric circles of meaning.[12]

Carlos Baker has also used the concentric circle image to describe the epic structure of the novel, and he too suggests that the bridge is at the center. But if we look at the adventure of the hero in the subjective world, the center of the concentric circle is Maria, or, more accurately, the sexual experience with Maria, and blowing up the bridge is only a reminder of the dangerous task existing in the objective world. The labels for the circles can be taken from some of the levels of experience treated in the novel, naming them from the widest, most obvious levels: political experience, religious experience, societal experience, primitive experience, and, finally, sexual experience, representing the core. The hero journeys through each level until he reaches the core, and finally returns. This journey is an even more difficult one than blowing up the bridge because the "enemy" is not so clearly defined. As a matter of fact, Jordan is partly his own enemy.

He is his own enemy primarily because of inexperience. Jordan is a novice in the ways of the subjective world. He has, through education and experience, become aware of the existence of man's material problems, but his cynical attitudes have been used as a device to protect himself from becoming emotionally involved with people. He has been well trained in his work, but he has not been trained for involvement. Thus we see that at the beginning he is less prepared for his spiritual journey than for his physical journey.

He knew how to blow any sort of bridge that you could name and he had blown them of all sizes and constructions. There was enough explosive and all equipment in the two packs to blow this bridge properly even if it were twice as big as Anselmo reported it. . . .[13]

The young man, whose name was Robert Jordan, was ex-tremely hungry and he was worried. He was often hungry but he was not usually worried because he did not give any impor-tance to what happened to himself and he knew from experi-ence how simple it was to move behind enemy lines in all this country. It was as simple to move behind them as it was to cross through them, if you had a good guide. It was only giving importance to what happened to you if you were caught that made it difficult; that and deciding whom to trust. You had to trust the people you worked with completely or not at all, and you had to make decisions about the trusting. He was not worried about any of that. But there were other things.[14]

Robert Jordan is obviously disturbed, but he is not worried about the tactical operation. Nor is he unduly concerned about death. As a human being, he is sometimes afraid, but it is made clear throughout the novel that he has already come to terms with his own death, at least on an objective level. He is somewhat concerned about being tortured and remains so throughout the novel. But still he is worried, and the omniscient author does not immediately reveal what it is that worries Jordan. We learn gradually that this is his fear of becoming subjectively involved with those with whom he must work. He will learn to care and will thus expose himself to the full pain of human relationships. Further, by becoming involved with others, he will have to confront himself and his relation to his past.

At first we learn that he is concerned not simply with his own death, but with the possibility that he may be forced to kill himself rather than be captured. We learn later that this is a vital concern since he has been unable to forgive his father for committing suicide. Even more important, we learn that the cynicism he has developed is a device to protect himself from emotional involvement with people and from resenting his job and the inequities of life. This protective shell is evident as he responds to Anselmo's truthfulness.

"It should be of the highest interest," Anselmo said and hearing him say it honestly and clearly and with no pose, neither the English pose of understatement nor any Latin bravado, Robert Jordan thought he was very lucky to have this old man and having seen the bridge and worked out and simplified the problem it would have been to surprise the posts and blow it in a normal way, he resented Golz's orders, and the necessity for them.[15]

For a moment, Jordan responds emotionally to the old man. Hurriedly, however, he assumes the objective and soldierly attitude. He subordinates himself and Anselmo to the cause and to the concept of duty.

And that is not the way to think, he told himself, and there
is not you, and there are no people that things must not
happen to. Neither you nor this old man is anything. You are
instruments to do your duty. There are necessary orders that
are no fault of yours and there is a bridge and that bridge can
be the point on which the future of the human race can turn.[16]

Jordan is a good, well-trained, efficient, properly loyal
but cynical soldier as he starts the journey. He believes, as
he tells the gypsy, that "in this type of work you have to
have very much head and be very cold in the head."[17] This
is the efficient and unemotional hero who will discover on
his journey that he and another human being can be "everything."

Jordan starts on his journey knowing the extreme importance of his role to the group he will work with. He
knows that Kashkin, a potential hero who had preceded
him on the journey, had become so emotionally involved
with himself that he had helped to destroy the unity of the
group. Though Kashkin had led Pablo's band on a successful mission, they had done nothing since.

At the outset, Jordan's spiritual journey parallels his physical journey. He is led to the threshold of the dark world,
and here he is challenged by Pablo; but in this journey
Pablo is even a more dangerous obstacle than in the physical journey. Pablo is not merely the leader of a band which
Jordan must use, a leader who is turning selfish and coward-
ly, he is the former hero of the early part of the revolution
who has now become Holdfast, the tyrant, the symbol of
the *status quo*. Further, at another level, he is the symbol of
the hostile father. Like Jordan's own father, Pablo will no

longer face up to the world and his responsibilities in it. Thus it is Anselmo, who in some ways has the pride and dignity and humanity of Jordan's grandfather, who at the beginning of the journey helps Jordan cross the threshold into the dark world. He interrupts Pablo's interrogation immediately after the point at which Pablo states his basic concern over Jordan's arrival. Pablo asks Jordan, "What right have you, a foreigner, to come to me and tell me what I must do?"[18]

Pablo perfectly understands the supplanting role of the hero. Jordan, himself, is not so aware of his role or his spiritual task. His mind is centered on his military duty, and he has not been trained for the deeds he will have to perform on the spiritual journey. But part of the hero's task is to learn, and Jordan learns on a variety of levels.

The first level is the world of politics. Jordan *had* been trained in politics. Some critics, over Hemingway's objections, have seen the novel primarily in terms of the development of Hemingway's political position, equating Jordan with Hemingway. In reality, Jordan's political position is described quite early in the novel. Any changes in his political philosophy have already taken place before the action of the novel begins. Through flashbacks, we learn about his initial political fervor and what has happened to it. When Jordan reminisces about his experiences, we learn that he had had the religious crusader's feeling, but now recognizes that at least in part he had been too naive. Foreign intervention, his association with the officers at Gaylord's and his talks with Carkov made it impossible for him to maintain any of his original purity of feeling.

. . . if the situation was now one which produced such a thing as Gaylord's out of the survivors of the early days, he was glad to see Gaylord's and to know about it. . . . But was it corruption or was it merely that you lost the naivete that you started with? Would it not be the same in anything? Who else kept that first chastity of mind about their work that young doctors, young priests, and young soldiers usually started with?[19]

For that matter, the political experiences of almost all of the characters are rather thin. For Pablo, the "Republic" is no longer strong enough to sustain his fears, to stop his worries about losing the material possessions he has gained. Agustin's political beliefs have solidified into personal hatred against a system and those responsible for it. Anselmo, believing still in the "cause," is more of a Christian and an anti-Fascist than a Communist. Both Pablo's and El Sordo's bands have deeper needs than can be satisfied by Communism.

Perhaps the best example of the ineffectuality of political belief is to be found in Joaquin. Even though he naively refuses to believe the derogatory stories told him about his idol, *La Pasionaria,* he finds that his political beliefs are not enough to support him against the approach of death. The majority of characters in *For Whom the Bell Tolls* have tried to reject religion for an almost religious belief in a political system. But the political belief does not furnish an adequate replacement for the emotional losses resulting from their denial of Christianity. When Joaquin, in his last moments, switches from the slogans of brotherhood to the religious "Hail Mary," it is a striking example of the emotional inefficacy of the political substitute.

The religious world is the novel's second level of experience from which Jordan must learn. Anselmo's attempts to weave his religious values into his newly adopted political creed serves, like Joaquin's reversion, as an example of the strength of this world. Anselmo is the hunter, and he is also the priest of a type of humanism that recognizes both the good and the evil in man. He reminds one of the priest in *A Farewell to Arms* in his desire to return home to the mountains where there is hunting and where people may live in peace and dignity through tradition. But he is willing to take an active part in the battle against Fascism even though he does not believe in killing. He is aware that, according to the new materialism, God is dead, and he knows that there must be something to replace the loss. For man is capable of much evil, and he must be able to atone for the evil he does. For most of the characters, then, the religious experience appears more deeply seated than the political.

But within this religious circle of experience is another that is even more basic. It might be called the societal experience. Though the action of the novel is limited to four days, *For Whom the Bell Tolls* offers an exceptional range of national characters. Robert Jordan, the foreigner, is an American. There are Germans, Frenchmen, Englishmen, Russians, and, of course, Spaniards. It is, however, impossible to neatly categorize the Spaniards as Spanish, for gypsies and Moors are among them, and the provincial characteristics of almost all the characters are described in detail. They become identified as people who are "from" a particular town or area, and their loyalties are to that area and their own people. These loyalties are frequently contrasted with each other through conflict.

The most basic societal loyalty is the one to the family, or tribe. No one in the novel illustrates this better than Pablo. He is the leader who, abdicating his responsibilities through fear, is almost destroyed by loneliness. Pablo's loneliness is different from Anselmo's, who feels lonely without prayer. Pablo has loneliness for people, and it is finally his feeling for the tribe that brings him back to the group against the bridge. When the bridge has been blown and escape becomes a necessity, he murders the helpers he has brought along. His justification, which silences Agustin's taunting questions, is "Shut up. . . . They were not of our band."[20]

In one sense, Jordan is only an observer at the tribal level of experience, and yet he can be used as a link between this area and an even more basic one. Although he does not belong to the "tribe" of Pablo, he becomes deeply involved with all of its members in those four days of association. He thinks of his own family relationships, of his connections with his father and his grandfather and the heritage that particularly his grandfather had left him. He becomes aware of an even more basic relationship which is connected with both the religious level of experience and the tribal, or societal. "Nobody knows what tribes we come from nor what our tribal inheritance is nor what the mysteries were in the woods where the people lived that we came from. All we know is that we do not know."[21]

Jordan's reference to the "mysteries" identifies that area
of "feeling" that is associated with superstition and magic,
or what we might call a primitive level of experience. Jordan must learn at this level also, and as he journeys into
the realm of the old mysteries, he makes associations with
magic and superstition, and he both thinks about and feels
the associations as he begins to learn that objective experience is no longer enough. For example, when he reflects
on the incident in which he threw away his father's suicide
gun, he realizes it was as though the physical action alone
were intended to silence his own fears that the gun had
some magical power to force him to destroy himself.

The "touching" ceremony is also a part of this primitive
area of experience. Anselmo is warmed by Jordan's slap on
the back after his long stay at his post during the snow-
storm. Later, Jordan is surprised by Pablo's handclasp.

> Robert Jordan, when he put his hand out, expected that it
> would be like grasping something reptilian or touching a leper.
> He did not know what Pablo's hand would feel like. But in the
> dark Pablo's hand gripped his hard and pressed it frankly and
> he returned the grip. Pablo had a good hand in the dark and
> feeling it gave Robert Jordan the strangest feeling he had felt
> that morning.[22]

There is, too, the necessity Jordan feels to touch the
lively squirrel just before the bombing begins. And there
are other references to primitive forces that are quite obviously in operation throughout the novel. The gypsy attitude toward the bear as a brother of man is compared to
the attitude of the American Indian early in the novel, and
frequently Jordan's own attitudes toward sex are more

magical than scientific. He wonders, for example, if the "powers" of his grandfather may have skipped a generation, and he refuses Maria's onanistic offer thinking, "I'll keep an oversupply of that for tomorrow. I'll need all of that there is tomorrow"—as though he could gain strength and courage from semen. Finally, Maria's temporary sexual inability the last night is interpreted as a bad omen. The sources of the primitive experience can ultimately be traced to the mysticism of Jordan's and Maria's sexual union.

It is not surprising that sex becomes more dominant the deeper one gets beneath the outer political surface of the novel, since it is the sexual experience with Maria that is the basis of Jordan's mystical experience. Strangely enough there has been much critical commentary on the amount of sex in this novel, although very little has been done to examine the relation of sex to the total structure. There has been a suggestion that sex was added in large amounts primarily to make the novel an attractive package for Hollywood. W. M. Frohock, in his *The Novel of Violence in America,* has said,

The obsession to write about sex has grown in proportion to the size of Hemingway's books; and it has become less appropriate as it has grown. . . . Finally in the Spanish novel Hemingway simply lets the war go hang during the intervals of the sleeping bag. I do not deny that there is some poignance in Jordan's experience. He has waited until the eve of death to discover a good thing, and having found it, must now lose it. But these entre-actes of the tragedy use up very nearly a quarter of the book. Here again, Hemingway's personal interests intrude upon the story; personality and basic discipline clash.[23]

Until Robert Lewis' *Hemingway on Love,* there had been no serious attempt to discover the relation to the rest of the novel of what many critics called the "sleeping bag" scenes. This is rather strange since it would seem that any subject which takes up one-fourth of a book would be well worth more than a cursory investigation. In the first place, whether or not Hemingway uses sex for the sake of art or for the sake of a personal obsession becomes a highly important question, not only for the study of Hemingway as an artist but also in any study of the discipline and integrity that Hemingway has so widely proclaimed for himself.

A recognition of Pilar's function in the novel is necessary for a complete understanding of the importance of sex to *For Whom the Bell Tolls,* for it is Pilar who forces Jordan and Maria together. Commenting on the scene in which Pilar tries to discover whether or not Maria and Jordan have achieved *La Gloria,* Lewis says, "If it were not for the pervading presence of a mythic dimension in the novel, this scene would be the merest sentimental claptrap."[24] The mythic dimension is there, of course, but Hemingway takes pains to provide enough preparatory material so that Jordan's reaction to Pilar can be understood and accepted. Pilar's role in *For Whom the Bell Tolls* is much like Sam Father's role in Faulkner's "The Bear"; she is a shaman who initiates a youth into a spiritual or mystical relationship. Sam Fathers, of course, by introducing Ike McCaslin to the woods, to hunting, and to the bear, opens a spiritual world that makes the boy capable of understanding relationships with the past and with the world around him. Pilar introduces Robert Jordan to a world that, as a teacher and a man primarily oriented to an objective analysis of life, he has not been aware of at all, at least not consciously. She capitalizes on those basic primitive impulses that he, like all men, carries over with him from past generations, and indoctrinates him into a spiritual world. Joseph Campbell points out that the function of the shaman is to make possible the relation of the individual not just to the family or to the tribe or to society as a whole but to the universe.[25] And that is precisely the main function of Pilar in *For Whom the Bell Tolls.*

Though it is unusual for a woman to act as a shaman, there is always the possibility that an older woman may function as one. As Professor Irving Hallowell has pointed out, "There is one loophole in native theory . . . [that only men can be shamans] that makes it possible for women to exercise such functions in exceptional cases. They may do so after menopause when they are considered to be much more like men."[26]

Certainly Pilar qualifies under this modification. There is within the novel a great deal of discussion of Pilar's age and, as a matter of fact, her resentment at having passed her productive years. She is described often in terms of her masculine attributes, and at one time she actually takes over the leadership of the tribe, deposing Pablo in her ascent. Also, there is enough of the gypsy sorceress about Pilar so that we can see, and Jordan can believe, that she has supernatural powers. Her knowledge of weather and nature leads him to believe in her understanding of the phenomenal world, and when she reads his death in his hand, he makes an attempt to be objective and to shrug off her interpretations, but inwardly he is very disturbed. His own "superstitious" qualities lead him to consider what she says, and at least to keep part of his mind open to her suggestions. Thus he is ready to accept, partly at least, her seeming clairvoyance in sexual matters. In her wisdom, she forces Maria into the sleeping bag in an effort to provide both Jordan and Maria with a basic human emotional experience that she knows can, and which actually does, become a mystical experience.

For a time Hemingway thought of giving the novel the title of *The Undiscovered Country*. An apparent reference for such a title occurs in *Hamlet*, where Hamlet describes death as the dread of afterlife.

> But that the dread of something after death,
> The undiscover'd country from whose bourn
> No traveller returns, puzzles the will
> And makes us rather bear those ills we have
> Than fly to others that we know not of?[27]

Yet, there is still another implication. The title could be concerned with another world which Hemingway protagonists had never glimpsed. This is a country that the naturalistic and objective Hemingway protagonists, including the Robert Jordan of the first part of the novel, had never journeyed into, and it is Maria who opens this new world to the hero, with the guidance of the shamanistic Pilar.

Vladimar Soloviev has written that, for the mystic

Love is important, not as one of our feelings, but as the transference of the very centre of our personal life. This is characteristic of every kind of love, but of sexual love preem-

inently; it differs from other kinds of love by greater intensity; greater absorption and the possibility of a more complete and comprehensive reciprocity; that love alone can lead to the actual and indissoluble union of two lives made one.[28]

Other critics have commented on the mysticism within *For Whom the Bell Tolls*, but without examining in detail its importance to the novel. Ray B. West, Jr., points out that in this novel Hemingway "accepted a form of mysticism similar to that of John Donne." And S. F. Sanderson sees the passage in which Jordan remembers erotic dreams of Harlow and Garbo as "an attempt by Hemingway to forestall the disbelief of those who do not or cannot accept the ideal perfection of the Jordan-Maria relationship. He is writing about something which is more properly assigned not to the romantic view of love but to the realm of the mystical, . . ."[29]

The need to forestall disbelief was essential since the result of the mystical experience is so important to the whole novel. The validity of the novel *depends* upon the validity of the emotional experience. The narrator records throughout the novel enough about what Jordan thinks about his sexual relationships that the reader should be aware that his experience with Maria is not just another "good thing," as Frohock called it. Jordan has had "good things"; that is, he has had sexual experiences with a number of women. But Jordan is concerned about his own reactions, and he comes to the conclusion that this is not just another good thing, that he is "truly" in love with Maria. She is his true love, his wife, his sister, and the daughter he will never have.

Maria may be compared to the good aspect of the Queen Goddess of the World whom the hero joins in mystical marriage as the ultimate adventure in his quest. The marriage traditionally takes place at the center of the cosmos. The Queen Goddess is described by Campbell as "the paragon of all paragons of beauty, the reply to all desire, the bliss-bestowing goal of every hero's earthly and unearthly quest. She is mother, sister, mistress, bride."[30] There may be a dark side to her nature, but Maria is not presented with this side. The dark side of the Goddess of the World, as we shall see, is represented by Pilar. Maria is not the temptress. She becomes the means by which Jordan manages to become the modern hero. The descriptive passages of this union between the hero and the goddess are possibly the most intense of the novel.

What frequently disguises the intensity of this experience is the superficial objectivity of Robert Jordan, and the willingness of most readers to accept what he says at its face value. To be sure, Jordan attempts to maintain an objective attitude, and at times he is fairly successful, but the new world of Maria is constantly intruding. Often he cannot be as objective as he says he is going to be, or as "cold" as Pilar thinks him. For example, in the passage frequently quoted to cite Jordan's objectivity (beginning "Because now he was not there. He was walking beside her but his mind was thinking of the problem of the bridge now. . . . "[31]), the gradual shift back into thoughts of Maria is often ignored. The shift begins even in the first paragraph. Jordan begins to worry and then, "Stop it, he told himself. You have made love to this girl and now your head is clear,

properly clear, and you start to worry." The paragraph
that follows has nothing to do with his precise plans for
blowing the bridge. It is concerned with his relationship
to the group and the overall plan of the bridge. "So now
he was compelled to use these people whom he liked as
you should use troops toward whom you have no feeling
at all if you were to be successful." In the next paragraph he
begins by thinking, "So you say that it is not that which will
happen to yourself but that which may happen to the
woman and the girl and to the others that you think of."
Then he begins an analysis of his political beliefs, but he
always returns to the girl Maria. Jordan is not so objective
as he tells us or as he tries to be.*

Jordan is introduced at night to the "undiscovered country" in the sleeping bag with Maria, but it is not until their
sexual experience during the day on the mountainside that
the union becomes completely mystical. Here they experience *La Gloria*. The description of sexual intercourse in this
passage emphasizes nature, and in particular the sun and
the earth. It is through the blending of the physical and
emotional experience of intercourse, and especially in the
narrator's attempt to describe *ingestively* the emotional

* As a matter of fact, it is worth noting that this mental monologue
actually covers eight pages in which there are thirty-nine paragraphs;
fifteen of these are devoted to the bridge and its relation to the
group or to the politics of war, twenty-one are devoted to Maria and
to Jordan's relationship with her, two can be counted as transitional
paragraphs, and one is primarily concerned with thoughts about
the shaman, Pilar. Only the first paragraph has any mention of the
specific demolition problem with which he is supposedly engaged.

qualities of the orgasm—through very Donne-like images—
that Jordan's naturalistic objectivity is lost. Thus the description of the orgasm is one which dislocates the par-
ticipants from both time and space, and transcends into
"up, up, up and into nowhere, suddenly, scaldingly, hold-
ingly all nowhere gone and time absolutely still and they
were both there, time having stopped and he felt the earth
move out and away from under them."[32]

The critics and parodists have attacked passages such as
this, but largely because they see them only as the workings
of a naturalistic writer, and because they have failed to note
the different direction Hemingway is taking in this novel.
Such passages, however, are basic to the novel's structure
and its course of action, for it is only after Jordan and Maria
together lose the concept of time and space that Jordan begins to bring his experiences together into a harmonious
relationship.

During the day, and in nature, the lovers have escaped
the limits of time and space, but as Jake Barnes and Frederic
Henry had pointed out, the night is another thing. The
next mystical union is at night, and this time the description of their lovemaking is in terms of bringing time into
the romantic moment. All is *now,* with the past and future
rolled into the now, just as the seventy hours of Jordan's
life with the group becomes his whole life. And just as all
is now, so all is one: "one and one is one."[33] The hero and
the goddess have conquered time and space and diversity.
They have become one, and they have returned from the
other country to Spain and Jordan's physical adventure. As
many critics have noted, the novel begins and ends with

Jordan lying face down against the earth, and in the final scene, feeling his heart beat against the "pine needle floor of the forest." At the end of this love scene he is also conscious of returning to the earth: ". . . one now on earth with elbows against the cut and slept-on branches of the pine tree with the smell of the pine boughs and the night; to earth conclusively now, and with the morning of the day to come."[34] This time there is no talk of "dying," and the scene has been developed to bring the two lovers back into reality. The union at night functions as a resurrection into life and into the day ahead.

After the first love scene, the rest of the novel is spent in bringing Jordan's new vision into harmony with all the areas of experience: primitive, social, religious and political. The most important lesson Jordan learns is an affirmation of what Harry Morgan is supposed to have discovered negatively—that a man alone does not stand a chance. Jordan finds that "he, himself, with another person, could be everything." That is the first stage, and then comes the recognition of his own humanity and his involvement with other individuals, with the tribe, with religious experience, and with political experience, the latter probably the least important of all except in very practical terms. Above all he finds that, as in the quotation from Donne, he is involved with all mankind. He has become intimately associated with the transcendental "all" and thus is prepared for his sacrifice at the end of the novel. He has reinforced his belief in the external world with his newfound belief in the existence of a previously undiscovered country, a world within, or as he expresses it:

That is in Madrid. Just over the hills there, and down across the plain. Down out of the gray rocks and the pines, the heather and the gorse, across the yellow high plateau you see it rising white and beautiful. That part is just as true as Pilar's old women drinking the blood down at the slaughterhouse. There's no one thing that's true. It's all true.[35]

But Robert Jordan's hero-deed is not so simple as might appear here. The journey into the subjective world is also closely related to the individual conflicts within the novel. The novel becomes charged with the mythical qualities of previous legends that now become part of the modern heroic adventure. Both the modern application and the archetypal qualities of Jordan's adventure can be discerned in Campbell's explanation of the symbol of the maiden.

The hegemony wrested from the enemy, the freedom won from the malice of the monster, the life energy released from the toils of the tyrant Holdfast—is symbolized as a woman. She is the maiden of the innumerable dragon slayings, the bride abducted from the jealous father, the virgin rescued from the unholy lover. She is the "other portion" of the hero himself—for "each is both": if his stature is that of world monarch she is the world, and if he is a warrior she is fame. She is the image of his destiny which he is to release from the prison of enveloping circumstance.[36]

Jordan's heroic journey is neither for power nor fame; it is to find meaning. Thus, Maria symbolizes his destiny. He learns much from Maria, as he tells her. He has rescued her from the "unholy lovers" by destroying her past and the memory of the rape. She is not the virgin, for our conception of life in the twentieth century is too realistic for purity. This is also one of the things that Jordan learns. Unlike Frederic Henry, who has rejected all beliefs because he has been exposed to the realities of life, Robert Jordan accepts a belief in mankind through his experiences, and especially through Maria. He is able to replace his early cynicisms with a belief in man with all his weaknesses.

In the tradition of the hero, Jordan also rescues Maria from the jealous father, for Pablo is a hostile father figure to Maria as well as to Jordan. He is sexually interested in Maria, as Pilar especially is aware. He is jealous of Jordan, not just because Jordan has come to blow up the bridge, but because Jordan challenges his reign in the country and because he sees Jordan as a potential rival for his "daughter." The relationship becomes even more complex when we recognize that Pablo also becomes symbolic of Jordan's father. He is bearded, and he allows himself to be "browbeaten" by his dominating wife. Jordan thinks it is necessary to kill this weak man on at least two occasions, just as he is attempting to kill the memory of his father. But he does not do it. Like a Hamlet, he is unable to find an appropriate situation for the killing. We are reminded even more of the Oedipal associations when the gypsy Rafael combines the Christian myth with the myth of Oedipus by suggesting that the old hero should be blinded and betrayed to the Fascists. Jordan himself is haunted by the archetypal overtones.

"Thou are a bicho raro," Robert Jordan said, not wanting to let it go; not wanting to have it fail for the second time; knowing as he spoke that this had all been gone through before;

having that feeling that he was playing a part from memory of something that he had read or had dreamed, feeling it all moving in a circle.[37]

Jordan is reliving the role of the hero, and his mind is flooded with mythology. In the myth Hemingway creates, however, Jordan is saved by his mystical union with Maria; he is saved from the patricide and the need for then having to blind himself in order to "see."

When Pablo returns to the group, Jordan allows him to resume his position as leader. The man's physical presence influences him when they shake hands just before the battle. Finally, after Jordan is wounded we find that he is willing to let Pablo assume complete authority for the escape. His confidence in Pablo has been restored. The scene in which Pablo and Jordan take leave of one another is in striking contrast to the earlier scene in which Jordan remembers his father's lack of masculinity as Jordan left for college.[38] In the final scene with Pablo, the father and son are reconciled in their adult masculine roles. Pilar, the mother figure, is willing to throw away all her household supplies so that Jordan may be given the pack horse. The supplies, as she tells Primitivo earlier, are "to make a life with," and her willingness to throw them away to save Jordan is symbolic of her willingness to sacrifice her future and the future "home" of the group for his safety. But Pablo will have none of this, and Jordan agrees. "Robert Jordan saw Pablo shake his head and he nodded at him."[39] Then Pablo bends his face close to Jordan, just as Jordan's father had bent his whiskered face toward him years ago. "The sweat-streaked, bristly face bent down by him and Robert

Jordan smelt the full smell of Pablo." At this leavetaking there is no embarrassment. In their discussion, it is clear that they speak as equals with a common respect for one another. There is a new confidence in Pablo. Jordan has in actuality helped restore the man to his former position.

"I think you would do better in the Republic," Robert Jordan said.

"Nay, I am for Gredos."

"Use thy head."

"Talk to her now," Pablo said. "There is little time. I am sorry thou hast this, Ingles."

"Since I have it—" Robert Jordan said. "Let us not speak of it. But use thy head. Thou hast much head. Use it."

"Why would I not?" said Pablo. "Talk now fast, Ingles. There is no time."[40]

Pablo has indeed been restored. The father's powers have returned, but the hero is unable to return to the world from the journey. He must remain behind.

The hero has also punished the dominating mother image. In doing so, he has resolved the aggression he has always had for "that woman" who made a coward of his father. Pilar quite obviously displaces Pablo as the leader of the tribe. She bullies him and humiliates him in front of the others, and she becomes extremely fond of Jordan. She is obviously physically attracted to Jordan and she is quite happy while the two of them are leading the group. She sends Maria to his sleeping bag and into the heather with him, but part of the reason she does this is to enjoy the experience vicariously.

In her witchery Pilar becomes like the "bad" mother part of Campbell's Goddess of the World, part of whose makeup is "(1) the absent, unattainable mother, against whom aggression is feared; (2) the hampering mother who would hold to herself the growing child trying to push away and (3) the desired but forbidden mother (Oedipus complex) whose presence is a lure to dangerous desire (castration complex)."[41] Although she is an imposing character, Jordan is too much in love with Maria to allow Pilar to dominate him. Towards the end of the novel he has himself replaced Pilar as leader of the group and has excluded her from the vicarious love relationship. As they are preparing to leave for the bridge the final morning, she acts like the perfect example of one of Jung's dual mothers. She tries to frighten Jordan by reminding him of her palmistry. Part of the reason for this is to still his fears through her expression of love and concern; at the same time, it is also unconsciously meant to disturb him, to remind him of the possibility of death, and thus to make him emotionally dependent on her. But Jordan is infuriated and gives her a tongue lashing. She is further vanquished by Pablo when he returns. She baits Pablo for leaving, even though she has relinquished her leadership to him. He warns her several times not to mock him but she continues. Finally,

> Pablo looked Pilar in the eyes again and this time he did not look away. He kept on looking at her squarely with his small, red-rimmed pig eyes.
> "Thou," she said and her husky voice was fond again. "Thou. I suppose if a man has something once, always something of it remains."

"Listo," Pablo said, looking at her squarely and flatly now. "I am ready for what the day brings."[42]

It has been pointed out that Pilar does not say goodbye to Jordan after he is wounded.[43] She offers him a horse, but she is so full of emotion that she cannot trust herself to speak. Jordan, however, does not give her much chance. He asks her to slit the trouser leg as she and Maria kneel by him. Then he tells her "Go." He pays no attention to her, almost deliberately.

"Vamonos," Pilar said. "Dost lack anything, Inglés?" She looked at him and shook her head.
"No," he said and went on talking to Maria.[44]

Pilar has been essentially excluded from the relationship. She has been forced back into a secondary position. Thus Jordan has preserved both Pablo's and his own ego against the weakening force of the "hampering" mother.

In a very large sense the hero has also restored himself. One of his major problems has been to relate himself to the father image. He had been fond of his father, but ashamed of the man's lack of masculinity. His father had killed himself with the grandfather's Civil War pistol. A law officer returns it to the young Jordan, telling him casually that he has shot it a few times and knows it is a good gun. Young Robert takes it to the pool, looks over into the pool like Narcissus, and holds the gun momentarily by the barrel before dropping it. The gun, suicide, his father, and "taking the easy way out" all become associated. He has left part of his masculinity at the pool. The gun association becomes clear when Maria, entering his sleeping bag for the first time, is frightened by the gun. He calms her fears, telling her it is only the gun.[45] Then he puts it behind him. On the second night he wears the lanyard of the pistol around his neck and has it ready when the Fascist cavalryman approaches the next morning. It is the pistol he could have used to wipe out the bad memories of his weak father by killing Pablo, but he holds it in both hands and kills the young Fascist. The thought of self-destruction remains with him, of course, until the end of the novel, but he has developed a different attitude toward it. The possibility of destroying himself is now no longer a theoretical consideration. He is in an impossible position. The best he can hope for is a quick death. He knows how the Fascists treat prisoners, and he knows that he will be tortured if taken alive. He thinks about killing himself. The rational part of himself presents some rather good arguments.

Listen, I may have to do that because if I pass out or anything like that I am no good at all and if they bring me to they will ask me a lot of questions and do things and all and that is no good. So why wouldn't it be all right to just do it now and then the whole thing would be over with?[46]

Jordan tries to think about the group, but the part of himself that wants to take the easy way out allies itself with his pain and his recognition that he is slipping away and that if he is captured he will be humiliated before he is dead. Finally, he stops the argument by subordinating himself to the group. *"And if you wait and hold them up even a little while or just get the officer that may make all the difference. One thing well done can make—"*[47] And the novel's final image is of Robert Jordan lying on the floor of the forest holding himself in, completely concerned about those with whom he has become involved. He has put himself aside and has accepted death or capture for the group.

What we have, then, in the novel is a myth in which the subjective or unconscious world is brought into relationship with the objective or conscious world. It is the myth of a modern hero, built on fragmented associations from a common mythology but in no way is it a reinterpretation or imitation. Jordan has learned through his union with Maria that he can subordinate his own ego enough to become "everything" with another. He has learned that a man cannot take the easy way out but that he must suffer. He has also learned from and influenced all the other characters. He has become totally involved in mankind and is willing to sacrifice everything for it.

This is not to say that Hemingway deliberately set out to create a new mythology. What he did was to tell a story as "truly" as he possibly could, and to create his first romantic hero. One critic has said that

Robert Jordan is Jake Barnes and Frederic Henry ten years more mature, which is to say, he is Hemingway himself, with all his retinue of paradoxical tendencies. He is the man who would tear down all extant morality and deny the worth of any human endeavor. But he is simultaneously the yearner for a better existence for mankind.[48]

Jordan is more mature, of course. He does yearn for a better existence. He does not, however, merely complain that the universe is too hostile. He understands that he must face pain and suffering and death in order to make that life better for others. Nor does he have an ideal concept of humanity. He knows of the ignorance and the cruelty, and even that men may enjoy killing. He also recognizes that he shares their strengths and their weaknesses. But he does not deny the worth of human endeavor. He insists that that is what human beings must do—work for good. He does not tear down but champions extant morality. As a matter of fact, the novel can be interpreted as a politically conservative statement in that the hero attempts to reestablish the old morality in a new social context.

If both God and man are dead, as Fromm suggests, then there seem to be two possible solutions to the contemporary problem. The first is to reestablish God. Hemingway obviously does not try to do this. The other answer is to reestablish man. Hemingway does this through a highly complex myth of the hero. Through the use of the omniscient author and a more "ingestive" technique of writing, Hemingway succeeds in expanding the hero's consciousness into an "undiscovered country" that, in a scientific age, has been largely denied. In Jordan's exploration of various levels of mythic-human experience, Hemingway has linked the heroic-deed of a man in the twentieth century with all of the history of mankind.

The result is a novel that is complex, meaningful, and as close to aesthetic perfection as Hemingway could make it. *For Whom the Bell Tolls,* it seems to me, stands somewhat in relation to Hemingway's other works as *Moby Dick* does to the rest of Melville's work. And, like *Moby Dick,* it is true enough to stand continued reinterpretation.

VI

ACROSS
THE RIVER
AND INTO
THE TREES:

The Tyrant HERO

TEN YEARS ELAPSED between the publication of *For Whom the Bell Tolls* and Hemingway's next novel, *Across the River and Into the Trees*. Rumor had it that Hemingway was spending most of his time after the conclusion of World War II working on his "big" book, a novel about the Land, the Sea and the Air. When the novel finally appeared, it seemed to be about something far less spectacular—a duck hunt and a romance in Venice, with a great amount of detail about a few people who frequented Harry's Bar and the dining room of the Hotel Gritti. Most of the reviewers and Hemingway aficionados attacked the novel with a bitterness that suggested they felt betrayed,[1] even though press releases made it clear that this was not the big book but only a substitute that Hemingway had put into the ring when he thought he might not have time to finish the big one. Even those critics who had more time to think before publishing their estimates reacted rather violently to the novel. Philip Young attacked it in his *Ernest Hemingway*,[2] and although Carlos Baker protected it, he saw it as fourth on his list of five Hemingway novels, finding it "as a work of art and artifice . . . generally superior to the novel of Key West."[3]

Critics have found that one of the greatest difficulties in evaluating this novel of a death in Venice is in disassociating the author from the protagonist. Philip Young suggests that "there has never been less distance between Hemingway and his hero. . . ."[4] and John Killinger thinks that *Across the River and Into the Trees* is "the most accurate spiritual autobiography of Hemingway that will ever be written."[5] The linking of the Hemingway hero to Hemingway is certainly a valid aspect of Hemingway criticism, but it is equally important to see the novel on its own terms, separated from Hemingway's statements and actions in his personal life.

One must start, then, from the position that Hemingway himself insisted upon, that Colonel Cantwell was *not* Ernest Hemingway. Colonel Richard Cantwell is the fictional creation of Ernest Hemingway; he is the second heroic protagonist that Hemingway creates. A. E. Hotchner states that once he and Hemingway and Gary Cooper were talking about future movie roles for the Hollywood star.

Ernest asked me what I thought might suit Cooper and I suggested Across the River and Into the Trees. *"Good idea," Ernest said to Cooper. "You'd just be playing Robert Jordan ten years older."*[6]

The statement is not quite so simple as it first sounds, for a man changes greatly in ten years and his role in society becomes quite different. This is especially true of the hero. A close look at Colonel Cantwell and the identification of his heroic role, and an examination of Hemingway's use of focus of narration in this novel will indicate, I think, that *Across the River and Into the Trees* does have a number of the merits assigned to it by Carlos Baker, and several more. The novel certainly ranks far higher than the haphazardly created *To Have and Have Not,* and in its complexity is in some ways more satisfying than the final heroic novel, *The Old Man and the Sea.*

But understanding Colonel Richard Cantwell is a more difficult task than it first appears. He is a new kind of Hemingway protagonist, although his prototypes may be found in the earlier novels. He is no longer the passive seeker after knowledge, although he learns a great deal in the course of the novel. Mostly, however, his ideas have already been formulated, and he is attempting to live by them, rather than to adjust his thinking to the experiences he goes through. Thus he is far different from Jake Barnes or Frederic Henry, and especially Robert Jordan. He is more closely related to Count Mippipopolous of *The Sun Also Rises,* or Count Greffi of *A Farewell to Arms.* Yet he is not quite like either one of these earlier characters, though he is, as they were, past the prime of life. Like Count Mip-pipopolous, he bears the scars of an active warrior life. Un-like the Count, however, no one can say of him that he is dead. The Colonel is still very much alive until his death at the end of the novel. As we see him in the novel his values are superficially like the Count's, and they have per-haps solidified to the same degree, but he uses them for an extremely active life. The Count enjoyed life passively, without becoming involved, and his value system served to isolate him from the subjective world. His "values" were both self-indulgent and self-protective. Cantwell, too, loves food and wine and beautiful women, and love has a place in his values. As a matter of fact, love for Renata and for "country" and for tradition seem to be his basic values. But he is engaged in living and is emotionally involved with people. Certain of his values may isolate him from at least a segment of the world, but the love he has for Renata, for example, is neither completely self-protective nor com-pletely self-indulgent.

He has to some degree attained the wisdom of the ancient Count Greffi, and he also maintains a rather strong belief in love as a religious feeling. Here again, however, there is a difference. He has not yet gained the serenity of the older Count. He is still very much alive physically, although he is dying, and he is mentally very much alive too.

Perhaps the "hero" that he most closely resembles at one level is Harry Morgan of *To Have and Have Not*. Or at least the animal vitality of Colonel Cantwell is somewhat like that of the protagonist of the Key West novel. He is often crude, truculent, inconsiderate. And he is also very individualistic. But there is one large difference in the two characters. Though both are wounded, bitter men, Colonel Cantwell has a system of values, a code of morality that is based on more than self-survival, and he is intelligent enough to make rational decisions and to analyze his own experience and see its relation to his own actions. He is also aware of the reactions of others to his statements and action, and he has a strong sense of responsibility and guilt. He is, then, a highly socialized creature with, to some degree, the animal cunning and suspiciousness of Harry Morgan. He is not, like Jake Barnes or Frederic Henry, the man that things happen to, with the exception of that one thing that happens to every man—death—which was denied to both Barnes and Henry within the confines of the novel.

There is one other character in Hemingway's novels whom Colonel Cantwell resembles more than any of the others, and this is Belmonte as he is pictured in *The Sun Also Rises.* Belmonte is old, and has lived his great moments. He is sick with a fistula, and he is not accepted by the crowd, but he is too self-contained to be affected by the crowd. "His jaw only went further out. Sometimes he turned to smile that toothed, long-jawed, lipless smile . . ." and at the end of the scene he goes "back into the ring."[7] He is the old hero, the champion who is being replaced by youth. But again, Cantwell is not quite like Belmonte because Cantwell does not impose conditions on the situation as Belmonte did. Belmonte chose bulls of a certain size and with horns not too dangerous. Cantwell has no choice in his situation, but he meets this externally imposed situation on its own terms. Both men face death stoically, although Belmonte no longer works as often in the terrain of the bull. Cantwell continues to work in the terrain of death. In this sense Cantwell is like a youthful Belmonte, or like the young Romero. But he is old, and he stands in relation to youth, in the form of Renata, much as Belmonte stands in relation to Romero and as Santiago stands in relation to Manolin in *The Old Man and the Sea*. Like Belmonte, however, and unlike Santiago, Colonel Cantwell has not yet learned to accept the inevitable with humility. Most important, we find that although Hemingway had treated characters of similar age and temperament he had never used such a character as the protagonist of one of his novels.

Robert Jordan was the young, the questing hero, but the re-created Hemingway protagonist is of another type. Although Hemingway could have suggested to Gary Cooper that Cantwell is just another Jordan ten years older, this does not mean that the man or the society has not changed in the interim. The society has changed, and the man has changed. As Joseph Campbell points out, "The hero of yesterday becomes the tyrant of tomorrow, unless he crucifies *himself* today."[8] If we continue to look at Cantwell as though he were Robert Jordan just as he was in *For Whom the Bell Tolls*, then we miss a great deal of the novel's point. The hero of *Across the River and Into the Trees* is no longer young or questing; he is older, and he has become "the tyrant of tomorrow."

Earl Rovit, in *Ernest Hemingway*, uses the terms "tyro" and "tutor" to identify two distinct types of Hemingway hero modelled after Philip Young's "Nick Adams hero" and "code hero."[9] Curiously enough, Cantwell to some degree fits both categories, but is not completely contained in either one. He is the tutor at times, but he is also the code hero. He learns a great deal from Renata, but she also learns from him, and he also religiously and rigidly adheres to a code that makes him sometimes an outspoken critic of all the younger generation except Renata. Thus he is in a sense something of a father figure, as many critics have commented.

So Cantwell is a different type of hero. He is neither the self-controlled and rather passive youth, nor the questing warrior, but a belligerent and irascible bull-like man of fifty years. Like Oedipus at Colonus, Colonel Cantwell in Venice complains about his treatment, rages against the fates, finds succor in a city he loves, attacks the younger generation and, in his own individualism, refuses to give way. But like Oedipus, he goes to his death with all the dignity and control that a man can bring to the act of dying. It is little wonder that with their expectations based on earlier heroes critics should have rejected Colonel Cantwell, for he is in reality a new type of hero—the tyrant. He is Ahab, who sees the world around him as the threatening whale, or he is Holdfast of the mythological world. As Joseph Campbell explains,

. . . the mythological hero is the champion not of things become but of things becoming; the dragon to be slain by him is precisely the monster of the status quo: Holdfast, the keeper of the past. From obscurity the hero emerges, but the enemy is great and conspicuous in the seat of power; he is enemy, dragon, tyrant, because he turns to his advantage the authority of his position. He is Holdfast not because he keeps the past but because he keeps.[10]

There are certainly rather obvious elements of the tyrant in Colonel Cantwell. Unlike the usual Hemingway hero, he is the champion of things past: he owes allegiance to old military ways, to an old city and its traditions, to a group of old World War I companions. Further, he wishes to keep. He is in love with the most beautiful of the young generation and he refuses to become the tutor to another representative of that generation.

Just as symbolic as Nick Adams' failure to recognize the landlady in the story "The Killers" is Colonel Cantwell's failure to recognize his driver. The Colonel thinks the driver is Burnham; he is not, he is Jackson, a man (or youth) of the same name as the man the Colonel will quote, and he is the driver who will carry him finally out of the city and across the river into death. Jackson is a member of the new civilian army and hardly oriented to the type of thinking that the Colonel respects. Jackson is passive. He reads comic books and sleeps, and does not have any fun (or at least the Colonel suspects he does not). Colonel Cantwell is contemptuous of him with a rather different contempt than he shows, for example, for the Fascists he outfaces or the sailors he thrashes. But Jackson too is a veteran. Jackson has faced the big death in a military blunder that he says he could not face again. Colonel Cantwell could have, and for a moment does, become the tutor for the boy, but he is too wrapped in his own code and too busy "keeping" to become the "tutor" hero. His war stories are not Jackson's war stories, and he recognizes the discrepancy between the two worlds and the two generations. He also recognizes his own irascible nature that keeps him from communicating with the soldier-driver. He is totally unlike Santiago in *The Old Man and the Sea,* who is patient and humble and who is able to care for and respond to a member of the younger generation.

Cantwell is unfair to Jackson frequently and without cause. When the two talk about art as they drive through the countryside, Jackson's love for "country" and for the paintings of the country should have appealed to Colonel Cantwell's own love of country. But for one thing the distance between the two men is too great. Cantwell is a colonel and (as Jackson rightly accuses him) often in his own mind is still the brigadier general. In a gesture of friendliness the Colonel shows Jackson the view of Venice with its historical content, and Jackson can only thank him for pointing it out. The "General" now interrupts his description with a bit of factual information about the pointed steeples. He has little patience. And when later they disagree about the definition of a "tough" town, the Colonel says, trying to be objective,

"O. K., Jackson. Maybe we move in different circles. Or maybe we have a differing definition for the word. But this town of Venice, with everybody being polite and having good manners, is as tough as Cooke City, Montana, on the day they have the Old Timer's Fish Fry."[11]

Here he attempts to be so specific that Jackson can have no retort, but Jackson does. He tells the Colonel what town *he* thinks is tough. And the Colonel must disagree with that. Finally, when they arrive at their destination the Colonel's personality changes to the "General" for no apparent reason.

> *"Is it okay to leave your gun and shooting gear in the trunk, sir?"* [Jackson asks]
> *"Sure. They don't steal here. I told you that once."*
> *"I wanted to take the necessary precaution, sir, on your valuable property."*
> *"You're so damned noble that sometimes you stink,"* the Colonel said. *"Get the wax out of your ears and hear what I say the first time."*[12]

Later Jackson thinks, "He sure is a mean son of a bitch, . . . and he can be so God-damn nice." Jackson has obviously been concerned about the car and the possessions in it. Colonel Cantwell tells him that they don't steal at the Hotel Gritti. Later, however, he chides himself for not keeping an eye on his luggage at the same hotel, and he even remembers a situation in which he caught an employee looking through his suitcase. Jackson's fears were not unfounded. It is just that the Colonel is too irascible to act as tutor. As Carlos Baker points out, Cantwell has the capability for pity, but the feeling usually comes *after* the situation that requires it.

Frequently the critics have implied that since this is a self-portrait rather thinly disguised, the writer pictures Cantwell with complete sympathy. This is not true. He can be mean and completely unfeeling, as Jackson points out, and with little excuse except the hypertension that Carlos Baker describes. But it is not just the hypertension created by the constant awareness of his closeness to death; it is a part of his personality that he often cannot control even while he is with Renata. He is partly an Ahab-like hero, or a Lear-type hero, or an Oedipus-type hero. Or he is the Ulysses of Tennyson's poem, hating the concept of change but finally accepting it.

In developing such a protagonist, Hemingway once more experimented with focus of narration. Remembering the initial attack on the novel, one can only conjecture wildly on the reception it would have had had it been written in the first person. The "I" would have been even more closely associated with Hemingway, thus making the novel more difficult to examine objectively. Further, passages that are reported by this strangely omniscient author might have sounded even more self-protective than they sound protagonist-protective in its present form. Hemingway's attempts to experiment with focus of narration in this novel result in a point of view that technically might be called a "limited omniscience," in which the omniscient author chooses to remain almost entirely within the scope of Colonel Cantwell's sphere of action and thinking. But on infrequent occasions the omniscient author chooses to tell us of other things that he wants us to know about the Colonel. For example, when the Colonel tours Venice in the morning, he buys some clams, and we find out something that the Colonel may know but does not necessarily think about at the time.

He drank the juice and cut the clam out, cutting close against the shell with the curved knife the man handed him. The man

*had handed him the knife because he knew from experience
the Colonel cut closer to the shell than he had been taught to
cut.*[13]

Hemingway as author wants us to know this information.
It has something to do with a peculiar excellence of the
Colonel; Cantwell is a perfectionist.

In the paragraph which follows we find another example
of this shifting point of view, an example which poses a
number of questions.

*The Colonel paid him the pittance they cost, which must
have been much greater than the pittance those received who
caught them, and he thought, now I must see the stream and
canal fishes and get back to the hotel.*[14]

The third-person narrator tells us that the Colonel makes
payment for the clams. That much is clear. Apparently he
also tells us that the pittance is much more, however, than
the pittance the people who caught them received for their
work. But is it really the omniscient author telling us this?
The next clause is, "and he thought, now I must see the
stream and canal fishes and get back to the hotel." What
has happened is that the omniscient author and the protagonist have been thinking along the same lines. The
omniscient statement is taken over by the Colonel's thinking, and he continues from that statement.

This is a consistent device that is most closely associated
with the narration in the more romantic central section of
the novel; that is, in that part of the novel that deals with
the Venetian adventures of Renata and Colonel Cantwell.

The much more naturalistic frame of the novel—the duck-shoot scenes which enclose the Renata-Cantwell relationship—is related much more objectively, especially in the first chapter. Chapter II, however, opens with just such a narrative device.

> *But he was not a boy. He was fifty and a Colonel of Infantry in the Army of the United States and to pass a physical examination that he had to take the day before he came down to Venice for this shoot, he had taken enough mannitol hexanitrate to, well he did not quite know what to—to pass, he said to himself.*[15]

In these two examples the device does not have too much import, but in other places it produces some rather startling results.

> *He saw the girl watching him and he smiled at her. It was an old smile that he had been using for fifty years, ever since he first smiled, and it was still as sound as your grandfather's Purdey shotgun. I guess my older brother has that, he thought. Well, he could always shoot better than I could and he deserves it.*[16]

In this passage we find first the objective reporting of two people smiling at one another. Then the omniscient author describes this smile in terms of the Colonel's past (it is evidently the smile he had as a baby, which at first seems ridiculous) and then in terms of the quality of the smile. The comparison here is to an expensive and soundly made hand-crafted weapon. But when the author states "your grandfather's Purdey shotgun" there is an indirect reference to the reader through the indefinite "you." And though the reader's grandfather may never have had a Purdey, the reference is still general enough (as in "as —————— as your grandfather's ————— —————") that the reader may feel directly addressed. And at this point the omniscient author, the reader and the Colonel are all operating at the same level, for the Colonel immediately picks up the reference and again completes the thought pattern. "I guess my older brother has that, he thought." Hemingway has apparently attempted to bring the reader, the omniscient author, and the protagonist of the novel all together at the same level of involvement. Ironically, the technique is not too dissimilar to the one Sherwood Anderson was attempting in *Dark Laughter* and *Many Marriages,* which Hemingway had satirized. Hemingway's attempt to decrease the reader's artistic distance from the work had been moderately successful, especially in *Green Hills of Africa,* but it was hardly suitable for the novel, and for this novel in particular.

Unfortunately, the result of this experimental approach is that superficially it seems to be an attempt on the part of Hemingway to justify his protagonist, to make him a more acceptably human character and to soften that harshness with which he views the world. It cushions his toughness or apologizes for it, thus giving cause for critics to attack the views of the protagonist as Hemingway's views. Further, the technique fails on occasions when the omniscient author tells us rather personal things about the Colonel, as during this internal monologue:

But how could she love a sad son of a bitch like you?
I do not know, he thought truly. I truly do not know.
He did not know, among other things, that the girl loved
him because he had never been sad one waking morning of his
life; attack or no attack. He had experienced anguish and sor-
row. But he had never been sad in the morning.[17]

Now this is rather unfortunate. It is the type of protection of the protagonist that deserves attack because it destroys rather than develops the novel. After close reading
one recognizes that there are qualities about the Colonel
that Renata certainly loves. She could not know, however,
that he has never been sad in the morning. She can only
tell from her association with him that he is not the type of
person ever to be sad in the morning. This is more precisely the meaning of the passage. She is in love with a
particular quality of the man, one that the reader can recognize from a number of passages in the novel. For the
omniscient author to tell this to the reader is an intrusion
of the worst kind. And these unfortunate intrusions are too
frequent, although Hemingway's attempts to bring the
reader and the protagonist together through the manipula-
tion of the omniscient author are sometimes successful.
When the technique is successful, the reader is scarcely
aware of what has happened; when it fails it fails so obviously that it conditions the reader's attitudes toward the
whole novel. More than anything else, Hemingway's failure in narrative perspective is what keeps the novel from
achieving artistic greatness.

Whether the technique fails or not, we know that at least

some attempt has to be made to soften for the reader the irascible temperament of Colonel Cantwell. Shakespeare, writing for the stage and with a historical rather than a contemporary hero, did not have the same problem with Lear. Hemingway's tyrant is a contemporary, and Hemingway had the problem of presenting a man who is unjust in such a manner that the reader could still be able to identify the heroic qualities behind what Carlos Baker has called his hypertension.

One other reason that critics have seen this novel as extremely biographical is that the protagonist is used for one of the most direct and vitriolic attacks that Hemingway ever made in the novel form or even in his nonfiction writings. For the things that Cantwell attacks are for the most part those that Hemingway as a nonfiction writer had also attacked. Thus there is a strong tendency to see Cantwell's diatribes against the world and the systems and modern civilization and modern warfare as attacks by Hemingway. It is especially difficult, therefore, to maintain an artistic distance from the author.

Unlike the method used by Joseph Conrad in *Victory* to achieve an aesthetic distance from his narrative by having Marlowe report what he had seen or heard, sometimes even at second and third hand, Hemingway often tries to decrease the aesthetic distance between the reader and the author, pulling the reader closer to the thinking of the character and the narrator. Especially in the major part of the novel rather than in the frame sections, a great deal of the narration offers the reader almost a direct confrontation of ideas. In several long passages the narrator merely introduces the situation, and then Colonel Cantwell's thoughts are presented as he (1) thinks to himself, (2) talks to Renata, or (3) talks to the picture of Renata. Unfortunately, unless the reader can maintain his own artistic distance from what he is reading, many of the ideas seem to be direct statements from Hemingway that he had already made public, and the narrator standing between Hemingway and the story is completely forgotten. Particularly is this true of the attack on the American writer whom Philip Young identifies as Sinclair Lewis. Hemingway had attacked Lewis before in *The Torrents of Spring,* and the narrator of the later novel attacks him personally. He attacks not only his writing but his physiognomy. Lewis had visited Hemingway in Cuba and felt that their old enmities had been forgotten. Apparently they had not.

They looked at the man at the third table. He had a strange face like an over-enlarged, disappointed weasel or ferret. It looked as pock-marked and as blemished as the mountains of the moon seen through a cheap telescope and, the Colonel thought, it looked like Goebbels' face, if Herr Goebbels had ever been in a plane that burned, and not been able to bail out before the fire reached him.

Above this face, which was ceaselessly peering, as though the answer might be found by enough well directed glances and queries, there was black hair that seemed to have no connection with the human race. The man looked as though he had been scalped and then the hair replaced.[18]

Philip Young says that in these attacks "the discipline which once kept Hemingway from the self-indulgence of chronicling his every opinion, taste and whim has broken down utterly."[19] It should be remembered, however, that most of the attacks are on ideas and institutions that Cantwell might very naturally have disliked. As the individualistic "fighting" general, he would have hated the "political" generals Eisenhower and Walter Bedell Smith. He has a hatred for the generals who sat behind the lines and planned the big plan without doing any of the fighting. They do not live with their troops as soldiers, but far behind the lines as politicians. Nor do they suffer as soldiers. Such generals, however, were necessary to modern warfare. Robert Jordan and even General Golz in *For Whom the Bell Tolls* hated the necessity for this type of command decision so far from the actual fighting, but they realized its necessity. Cantwell, too, knows but cannot accept it. He is too much the old-fashioned infantry general officer with all of the prejudices of the military mind. He does not like the cavalry because it is not the infantry, although he explains that cavalry aren't any good because they have no place in modern warfare. At the same time he dislikes the air forces and the way they are used. He reconstructs old battles where infantry played the major role, and everything else becomes for him like "Fate" that he cannot control. And he becomes bitter about this Fate. The tyrannical ego in him that even he recognizes cannot come to terms with it. Sometimes he recognizes how unjust he is in his attacks. For instance, he speaks of himself as not the "lionhearted" but the "crap-hearted, . . . the unjust bitter criticizer who speaks badly of everyone."[20] And he does speak badly of almost everyone, but the reader should be aware that his attacks are the result of his own recognition that he is outmoded.

He sometimes speaks badly of the American soldier in World War II. He remembers that when he fought in World War I he spent a great deal of time during rests looking for water or looking for ditches to rest in safely. Yet after he has had a heart attack he vocally turns against the World War II soldier. "I can rest on my feet, or against a God damned tree. My countrymen sit down, or lie down, or fall down. Give them a few energy crackers to stall their whimpers."[21] Then he turns his attack upon the generals' wives, and bacteriological warfare, and the singing voice of Margaret Truman. But his attacks are at least partly explained by the omniscient author.

The Colonel, who was four star general now, in his wrath and in his agony and in his need for confidence, but secured temporarily through the absorption of the tablets, said, "Ciao, Domenico," and left the Gritti.[22]

It is to be remembered that he thinks well of the American GI in a calmer moment. "But we've got some good ones, too,"[23] he says.

And though he criticizes America, at one point saying, "The Hell with anything American except me,"[24] he and Renata plan a trip to the American West, just as Robert Jordan and Maria had. Renata spends some of her evenings planning the trip with materials that the Colonel has sent her. Strangely enough for the Baedecker-hating Colonel, the materials he has given her are the tourist guides put out by the AAA.

He attacks falseness wherever he finds it. He contrasts the American woman and her habit of sleeping with her hair in curlers and wearing padding in her brassiere with Renata's natural beauty and natural figure. He is proud that she refuses to become enamored of her own beauty and thinks of it only as a gift for her man. Especially when Cantwell speaks of his "ambitious" wife, the attack seems a personal attack by Hemingway on Martha Gell-horn. But it is also true that one of the dominant criticisms of American women that resulted from the American soldier's association with European women during and after World War II concerned the American woman's attitude toward herself and toward her husband. Cantwell wishes to keep the traditional concept of man's patriarchal status. Thus Cantwell's attack is consistent, and his overgeneralization is in line with his "General" manner.

As a military man he hates those who have profited from a war without having experienced the physical and mental suffering that war causes. He hates those who sold the American army raincoats that failed to shed rain, just as he hates the *pescecani,* the Milanese civilians who are also war profiteers. Nor is he so blind from his love of the army that he does not know that army officers have contributed to this type of dishonesty.

Whatever he attacks there seem to be one or two constants upon which the attack is based. First is his own high sense of morality. Second, he attacks those aspects of the life of others that make them demand less from life than he does. He is, as the omniscient author has told us, never "sad" in the morning. He faces each day with a vitality and expectancy that only the true romantic might have. To re-phrase Thoreau, "Morning is when he is awake and there is a dawn in him."[25] Certainly one of the most interesting aspects of this novel is the "dawn" view and the conflict be-tween the dawn and the dark. The man who is just about to die is one of the most youthful characters in the novel. Part of this "youth" is the Colonel's concept of life, which the point of his satirical attacks makes most clear. He is offended morally by Jackson's failure to live. To the Colonel, Jack-son's refusal to see outside his own limited world of sleep and comic books is a denial of life. At one point he "orders" Jackson to have some fun. Very early in the novel we see a good example of the dawn-of-life concept. The Colonel has taken medicine (mannitol hexanitrate) to the point where the examining doctor tells him that "They ought to make you drag a chain like a high-octane truck."[26] But be-cause of these preparations Cantwell passes the examina-tion. The doctor now wants to discontinue the farce and begins to question Cantwell about his health. Finally, the Colonel invites the doctor to the duck-shoot. And in this passage several distinctions are made. First, there is a sec-tion devoted to the discrepancy between their ages. They are members of different generations. The doctor then says that he is a city boy and that he can't even shoot. This makes little difference to the Colonel, since he suggests that no one else in the army can shoot either. Finally, the real distinction is made in terms of their contrasting attitudes toward life. It starts early in the passage, but begins to be quite apparent when the Colonel questions him about scientific research.

"I'll give you something else to back up what you're using."
[the doctor says]
"Is there anything?"
"Not really. They're working on stuff, though."
"Let 'em work," the Colonel said.[27]

Too concerned with living actively to pause and wait for medical science to arrive at some solution to his heart problem, the Colonel is completely disinterested in living on hope for a more secure future. He is not willing, then, to sacrifice *life* for the hope of existence. The idea becomes even clearer later.

"Go to hell," the Colonel said. "You sure you don't want to go?"
"I get my ducks at Longchamps on Madison Avenue," the surgeon said. "It's air-conditioned in the summer and it's warm in the winter and I don't have to get up before first light and wear long-horned underwear."
"All right, City Boy. You'll never know."
"I never wanted to know," the surgeon said. "You're in good shape, Colonel, sir."[28]

The Colonel is in good shape, comparatively. He is at least in the world of the awake, unlike the doctor who does not want to experience life. The doctor may wish to study it, to belong to that group which wishes to find ways to increase existence, but he does not want to join the Colonel in living life to the fullest, especially if it means making an effort and being uncomfortable. The Colonel, at the other extreme, is a romantic, and he hates anything that does not have the quality of bigness to it. This is why he attacks President Truman and Margaret Truman's voice. He conceives of Truman as a "little man," a failed haberdasher. "We are governed by the dregs of society," he tells Renata. He dislikes Margaret's voice because it is "thin," lacking in power. It is not the "big" voice. Cantwell's concern is for living in the grand manner, and not being "asleep" to the possibilities of life. This does not mean that he is an eternal optimist. The world is not beautiful just because man awakes to it. He tells Renata, "Every day is a new and fine illusion. But you can cut out everything phony about the illusion as though you would cut it with a straight-edge razor."[29]

It is easy enough to recognize that Cantwell is full of his own illusions. Sooner or later, however, he usually gets back to the truth of a situation. He is bitter about the loss of his division and he mentally castigates all those of the higher echelon who are responsible for it. One of the reasons that he must remain bitter, as he tells himself, is so that he will remember it. And he is not unaware that he too can make mistakes. "And what about that company dead up the draw? What about them, professional soldier? They're dead, he said. And I can hang and rattle."[30] He is his own skeleton in his own closet. Colonel Cantwell's tyrannical mind attacks a world that is making his way of life obsolete.

We are again dealing with the romantic hero in this novel. He is Holdfast, or Lear, or Ulysses looking at a changing world and a changing concept of life. And he is always true to his own concept of what life is. Most important, he will do nothing to reduce the possibilities of his own death. In fact, there is almost a suicidal desperation in Cantwell's activities during the weekend in Venice. As Carlos Baker and others have noted, there is for Colonel Cantwell much of the hypertension that Jordan experienced in *For Whom the Bell Tolls*, knowing that he might die at the blowing of the bridge. Everything has a particularly strong sense of life for the Colonel during these long days. He knows that he will die soon, and so does Renata. By protecting himself he could survive longer, but he has become involved in a situation that is disastrous for the one he loves, and he chooses not to commit suicide but to live as strenuously as he can to hasten the solution to the problem. As Robert Lewis notes, Cantwell's youthful mistress has become pregnant, and the only way that he can arrange for her continued happiness is through his own death. The two lovers never discuss the arrangement openly. They do not wish to intrude this trouble into what possibly is their last weekend together. But the arrangements are carefully and subtly made, so subtly that the reader often loses the thread of the developments. Renata introduces the subject rather tentatively.

"Will you marry me and will we have five sons?"
"I will! I will."
"The thing is that, would you?"
"Of course."
"Kiss me once again and make the buttons of your uniform hurt me but not too much."[31]

As we have learned earlier, she has already made a decision not to marry the Colonel under any circumstances, but she wishes to know whether he will marry her. With this emotional security she tells him indirectly of her pregnancy that will cause a change in their relationship and possibly even end it.

> They stood there and kissed each other true. "I have a disappointment for you, Richard," she said. "I have a disappointment about everything."
>
> She said it as a flat statement and it came to the Colonel in the same way as a message came from one of the three battalions, when the battalion commander spoke the absolute truth and told you the worst.
>
> "You are positive?"
>
> "Yes."
>
> "My poor Daughter," he said.
>
> Now there was nothing dark about the word and she was his Daughter, truly, and he pitied her and loved her.[32]

He pities her particularly because she has already announced another decision that she has made during the week, recognizing that he is going to die.

> "How is your mother?" he asked, lovingly.
>
> "She is very well. She does not receive and she sees almost no one because of her sorrow."
>
> "Do you think she would mind if we had a baby?"
>
> "I don't know. She is very intelligent, you know. But I would have to marry someone, I suppose. I don't really want to."

> "We could be married."
>
> "No," she said. "I thought it over, and I thought we should not. It is just a decision as the one about crying."[33]

This is after she has made him promise to do his best not to die, a promise he breaks on the duck hunt. As the novel progresses, the reader becomes aware, along with the Colonel, of whom she will marry. The Barone Alvarito finds them at the Gritti, and he tells the Colonel about the hunt. When he leaves, Renata comments,

> "We knew each other as children," . . . "But he was about three years older. He was born very old."
>
> "Yes. I know. He is a good friend of mine."[34]

Then the Colonel and the *Gran Maestro* discuss wines and what they used to drink in the old days and conclude the conversation by returning to the problem of dessert.

> "What do you want for the end of the meal?"
>
> "Cheese," the Colonel said. "What do you want, Daughter?"
>
> The girl had been quiet and a little withdrawn, since she had seen Alvarito. Something was going on in her mind, and it was an excellent mind. But, momentarily, she was not with them.
>
> "Cheese," she said. "Please."
>
> "What cheese?"
>
> "Bring them all and we'll look at them," the Colonel said.
>
> The Gran Maestro left and the Colonel said, "What's the matter, Daughter?"
>
> "Nothing. Never anything. Always nothing."

"You might as well pull out of it. We haven't time for such
luxuries."

"No. I agree. We will devote ourselves to the cheese."

"Do I have to take it like a corn cob?"

"No," she said, not understanding the colloquialism, but
understanding exactly what was meant, since it was she who
had been doing the thinking. "Put your right hand in your
pocket."

"Good," the Colonel said. "I will."[35]

At this point they return to talking about the war, and
Renata takes the distress from the situation by promising
that they will ride in the cold wind in the gondola after
they discuss the war.

The Colonel quite obviously has understood. But he becomes even more sure of her decision and the certainty of
it in a later conversation. The next morning she asks him
about the shoot.

"Don't you think I should go to the shoot?"

"No. I am quite sure. Alvarito would have asked you if he
wanted you."

"He might not have asked me because he wanted me."

"That's true," the Colonel said, and pondered that for two
seconds. "What do you want for breakfast?"[36]

It is after this scene that he begins to add another adjec-
tive to his descriptions of her. "You good, brave, lovely
girl," he calls her. But before he dies he must be sure that
everything is understood and that Renata's future, and their
child's future, is secure. He discovers this in three scenes

at the end of the book. The Barone waits for him at the lodge, and they discuss the hunt. Finally, the Colonel changes the nature of the conversation.

"I'm sorry you came so far for so few ducks."

"I always love the shoot," the Colonel said. "'And I love Venice."

The Barone Alvarito looked away and spread his hands toward the fire. "Yes," he said. "We all love Venice. Perhaps you do the best of all."

The Colonel made no small talk on this but said, "I love Venice as you know."

"Yes, I know," the Barone said. He looked at nothing. Then he said, "We must wake your driver."[37]

Then the Barone explains the surliness of the Colonel's boatman. The boatman, like himself, has been over-liberated. The Moroccans had raped the boatman's wife and daughter.[38] Thus it is natural that the Barone's friendship for the Colonel should contain the amount of enmity we see in Chapter XLIV, a chapter completely devoted to the leave-taking of the Barone and the Colonel. Cantwell insists that the Barone give Renata his love. Then he asks the Barone to tell Renata to pick up the portrait at the Gritti. In the final scene between the two, the Barone refuses to see Cantwell as anything but a colonel.

"Ciao, my Colonel. If one can say ciao to a Colonel."

"Consider me not a Colonel."

"It is very difficult. Good-bye, my Colonel."[39]

But all this is enough for the Colonel. He knows that

both he and the Barone were talking about Renata, not Venice. When, just before his death while making his peace with the world, he lists all of the things he has failed to do, he is sure that this situation has been properly taken care of. His life has not been completed successfully, as he notes. There are many things left undone. He catalogs them: he has killed enough ducks for the boy and his wife to eat, but not enough for a quilt; he has forgotten to give the dog Bobby the sausage he bought especially for him; he has not written a note to Renata. He also forgets that he had not provided the old man with a new engine for his boat. Like a new heart, this was an impossibility. After he admits to himself that he is no longer of use to the Army he remembers Renata and her situation.

You have said good-bye to your girl and she has said good-bye to you.
That is certainly simple.
You shot well and Alvarito understands. That is that.[40]

And that *is* that. The Colonel has discharged his major obligations and can now die properly, as he does by closing the door "carefully and well." This is not, of course, to suggest that he has fulfilled all his minor obligations. The one he fails to mention in his summary is perhaps the most important of them all. As Carlos Baker points out, when Renata chooses the boat with the old incapacitated engine, she is symbolically choosing the Colonel. It is her last gesture of love to him, and his failure to replace that engine, or to comment on that failure in the summary, is indicative of his recognition of her gesture. For his heart is of necessity being replaced by another's even though she says she would rather not.

We have, then, the death of another romantic hero, but this time it is the tyrant hero dying. He has performed heroic deeds throughout the novel. He has not only out-faced some Fascists but he has, with the young maiden watching from a distance, defeated two sailors in physical combat. Like the true "King" hero figure, he has van-quished them by himself.[41] He has also quite obviously proved himself as a lover. He is still the hero, but the prob-lem is that he is Holdfast—he is still trying to *keep*. He is wise enough to know that he has been replaced, that he is outdated, and he fights against the imminence of death until he becomes aware that only through his own death can there be room in the world for Renata and her child. He suddenly understands that the ego of the tyrant must be destroyed in order that new generations may live. He ac-cepts his own mortality on one level by overexerting as he poles his boat through the ice. He has symbolically helped the boatman pole him across to death. At the same time he has left behind him a pregnant Renata. He has left some-thing physical behind him; more important, he has left the spiritual aspect of his personality with Renata. He has pre-served for her the memory of him as the "pelagic fish," the romantic hero who not only performed acts of heroism but also allied himself to the old warrior traditions and then suffered the guilt from his lies (four, he counted) and his mistakes (three, he tells her). He bears the wounds openly that are symbolic of those human errors. He has never been the small man. The Colonel is like both the lobsters and the bonito that he sees in the market; he is not, as most men are, like the sole.

. . . the heavy gray-green lobsters with their magenta over-tones that presaged their death in boiling water. They have all been captured by treachery, the Colonel thought, and their claws are pegged.

There were the small soles, and there were a few albacore and bonito. These last, the Colonel thought, looked like boat-tailed bullets, dignified in death, and with the huge eye of the pelagic fish.

They were not made to be caught except for their voracious-ness. The poor sole exists, in shallow water, to feed men. But these roving bullets, in their great bands, live in blue water and travel through all oceans and all seas.[42]

The Colonel does not, like most men, travel in the shal-low water, but in the deep water of experience. He dies and finds his own immortality in death, too, by becoming part of the soil in the great continuum, just as the prawns find their own immortality by having "their shucked carcasses float out easily on an ebb tide on the Grand Canal." But in his life he has been the deep-sea fish, and the only thing that has "captured" him has been the treachery of life, which has not destroyed him but only made him fight more strongly to maintain his individuality.

Treachery is constantly under examination in the novel. Life is treacherous, and so is the relationship between man and woman. Like the deep-sea fish, the Colonel is caught by his own voraciousness and vitality, and like the lobster, he has been trapped often by the treachery of life. He has been trapped by fate, by decisions that have been made for him to follow, and by his own weaknesses, including the treachery of his own heart. And he does admit them as weaknesses. He made three wrong decisions, all three when he was tired, but that was no excuse and he does not ask to be excused. He has the hand to symbolize his human failures, a pegged claw that has not totally healed. But as Renata knows, it is a real hand, his human hand. And it is Renata, of course, who orders the lobster in tribute on the evening of their first night together.

The Colonel is always aware of the treachery involved in human relationships. He hears the decoy hen calling the drakes and leading them to their deaths. He notices that it has become too cold for the hen to employ treachery, and she switches to looking for security. Although Cantwell has just contemplated the "miracle" of his and Renata's love, he considers the hen, and for a moment thinks,

You bitch, . . . Though that is unjust. It is your trade. But why is it a hen calls better than a drake. You ought to know, he thought. And even that's not true. What the hell is true? Drakes actually call better.

Now don't think of her.[43]

But he does think of her, and he reconsiders. He recognizes that she would have climbed up in the tumbril with him. "Very rough trade," he says, thinking of Renata and her loving and being left now, like the duck, to find her own security. He has little regret as he closes the car door. He has been, as a romantic hero and as Renata has told him, a "good man." He has balanced his books, and he remembers the good-bye and knows her decision, but he also remembers her choice of the boat with the "old heart."

Lord Raglan has pointed out that there is nothing in the death of the hero that suggests defeat, and that the death "never takes place within the city."[44] Colonel Cantwell chooses his own place to die outside the city he has loved. The tyrant hero, in fact, can only remain the hero by recognizing the need for his own crucifixion. That is Cantwell's victory. He has made a place for the new hero, one who appreciates all of the things the Colonel has appreciated. The replacement will not be as vital and dynamic, but that is part of the victory too. The ways of the world and systematic fate, however, are strong. Even after death they confound his plans. He writes an order that the portrait and the shotguns he has with him shall be returned to the Hotel Gritti where they may be claimed. He cannot know that General Jackson's unromantic namesake will make the final ironically valid statement. "They'll return them all right, through channels." This is as effective a conclusion as the ironic scene with the tourists at the end of *The Old Man and the Sea*. It is, after all, the army way that Jackson is suggesting, a way that the Colonel has accepted as his life. Further, Jackson shows no understanding of the symbolic importance of the portrait of Renata and the shotguns of the Colonel. Finally, the narrator's inclusion of Jackson's cryptic remark is reminiscent of that unromantic truth that the young romantic idealist Holden Caulfield, in Salinger's *Catcher in the Rye*, cannot face—the fact that no matter how heroic a man's life, someone with no understanding will scrawl obscenities on the gravestone.

Perhaps Hemingway, like Melville, felt that he had written a wicked but great book when he had finished *Across the River and Into the Trees*. For the Colonel does not convert to Christianity at the end. His stoicism prevails, and his fight with the gods has been a bitter one. He has not become humble, but has battled death by living fully without any backtracking, and he has chosen his own time to die. His decision to leave Renata to the Barone is a sincere decision that is parallel to what Lady Brett Ashley explains as her reason for leaving Romero. As a sacrificial act it is "what we have in place of God." Especially when the hero chooses the time of his own death does he act in a God-like manner.

It is little wonder, then, that Hemingway was hurt and baffled by the adverse critical reception the novel initially received. He must have thought that his shift in narrative technique, the dreamlike quality of the Renata story, and the irascible hero would have pointed up the romantic qualities, and that the novel would be considered in these terms. But critics and readers generally expected the novel to be another installment of the story of the "progressive Hemingway hero" and reacted with surprise and an insufficient understanding of the tyrant-king qualities of Colonel Cantwell. As a result there was a general condemnation of this novel, which is, with the exception of what contemporary readers consider to be a failure in narrative perspective, one of the tightest, most artistically controlled of all of Hemingway's novels. In its symbolism, complexity and consistent portrait of the tyrant hero, *Across the River and Into the Trees* ranks with the best of Hemingway's works.

VII

THE OLD
MAN AND
THE SEA:

The HERO as saint and sinner

THE LAST "NOVEL" to be published during Hemingway's lifetime was *The Old Man and the Sea,* a work which
Hemingway would identify as a new form. The precise
generic classification is more or less inconsequential
although it is apparent that the work is a completely developed fable in the form of a very short novel. The protagonist of the book brings to full circle Hemingway's use
of the mythic hero, for Santiago is again a hero with a different face. He is a modern adaptation of what Joseph
Campbell has called the "saint or ascetic, the world-renouncer."[1] The true world-renouncer, Campbell explains,
follows a pattern

*of going to the father, but to the unmanifest rather than the
manifest aspect: taking the step that the Bodhisattva re-*

nounced: that from which there is no return. Not the paradox of the dual perspective, but the ultimate claim of the unseen is here intended. The ego is burnt out. Like a dead leaf in a breeze, the body continues to move about the earth, but the soul has dissolved already in the ocean of bliss.[2]

Like the Bodhisattva, Santiago too renounces the final step and returns to the world. After having successfully battled against the gods and won, the modern hero finds that he can return only after a torturous and defeating experience that strips him of everything except the symbol of his victory.

The Old Man and the Sea is simply told, and critics have almost universally acclaimed it. It is the story of an old but proud fisherman, Santiago, who had once been a champion fisherman but who has had no luck at all in eighty-four days. For the last forty-four of those days he has had to fish alone because the boy Manolin, his apprentice, has been forced by his parents to go with another fisherman. Santiago goes alone and ventures too far out into the sea. He catches a great marlin that pulls him out even farther. After a long struggle he kills the great fish, lashes it to the side of his boat, and starts for home. Sharks attack and eat the fish despite all the old man's efforts to keep them off. Santiago finally returns to his home port defeated, with only the skeleton to symbolize his victory. His apprentice, however, is so impressed by his heroic defeat that he chooses to disobey his parents and take the old man with him during the rest of the fishing season.

As Earl Rovit has pointed out:

Within the frame of the general interpretation of this story, there are many possible special readings; for Hemingway has so successfully narrated a journey and a return that almost any "incommunicable" experience may be suggested to the reader. The travail can be seen as a religious one, an introspective one, or an aesthetic one.[3]

Earl Rovit has specifically identified the novel as the journey of the "quest" hero, but it is important that the journey does not follow the typical pattern of the archetypal hero in his quest.

In many respects the story calls forth the basic quest pattern, such as in the myth of Jason and the Golden Fleece. But instead of a young man, the hero is an old fisherman. After many trials the hero attains his reward, but is then beset with vicissitudes as he tries to bring the boon back to mankind. Jason, through the help of the gods, is able to return with the Golden Fleece. Santiago is able to return only with the skeleton of his success. The major differences, then, are the ages of the heroes and the final results of their expeditions. In a detailed examination of the story of Santiago it becomes evident that there are also a number of shifts of emphasis and a number of differences from the typical quest that become important. And what becomes obvious, I think, is that *The Old Man and the Sea* is essentially a story of defeat. As a fable, however, it also suggests the potential of man despite inevitable defeat.

Because it is a fable it cannot be interpreted quite like, say, one of the bullfight stories, "The Undefeated," or the boxing story, "Twenty Grand," as Sheridan Baker does in finding the novel a story of "undefeat." The journey is not just a realistic battle with a big fish nor one in which a man tests his integrity against great odds; it is a romantic attempt on the part of a champion to test the gods of the universe; perhaps it is even an attempt at regeneration. What it finally becomes, however, is a statement about the "burning out" of the ego in the godlike attempt and the ultimate defeat on the way back to the community of men.

The quality of fable is introduced early in the work, not only through the omniscient author's description of the old man, but in the description of the comparative serenity of the man's existence. Santiago is well-loved by almost all around him. He has been unlucky for almost three months, but his community still favors him. Although there are people who laugh at him, most of the fishermen are sad about his loss of luck, and the boy is thus able to provide him with food gathered from the community of friends. But as the old man notes, the situation has been reversed from the time when Manolin was young. Then, he took care of the boy. Now, the boy arranges for his food and his bait.

The narrator of this story is perhaps even more charitable toward his hero than is the narrator of *Across the River and Into the Trees*. From the opening description of Santiago, which ends with a statement about his eyes which are "the same color as the sea and were cheerful and undefeated," we are aware that the narrator has taken a protective and sympathetic attitude toward the old man. This is not, for example, like the objective description of the bullfighter in "The Undefeated." But as we gradually learn more about Santiago, a number of things become clear that have been partially hidden by the omniscient narrator's early descriptions. For one thing, it becomes clear that Santiago feels superior to other men. At one time in his life he had competed in hand-wrestling. He had been the champion, but he gave up the sport when he decided that he could defeat any other man in that type of contest if he wanted to badly enough. For another, Santiago has little connection with the community of men. He has lost his wife and has no real involvement with another human being other than his disciple Manolin. He reads about the exploits of Joe DiMaggio and dreams of the irresponsible and kingly lion cubs playing on the beach. He discusses baseball with Manolin and has obviously told the boy about his own youth along the African shores. Typical of the young, however, the boy is impatient with Santiago's recapitulation of the "old times," for he reminds him that he has heard these stories. But the boy has faith in the old champion, and Santiago tries to restore that faith.

With the aid of the boy, Santiago is ready to go out to the sea on his archetypal quest. His conception of the sea is feminine, and thus regenerating.

He always thought of the sea as la mar which is what people call her in Spanish when they love her. Sometimes those who love her say bad things of her but they are always said as though she were a woman. Some of the younger fishermen, those who used buoys as floats for their lines and had motorboats, bought when the shark livers had brought much money, spoke of her as el mar which is masculine. They spoke of her as a contestant or a place or even an enemy. But the old man always thought of her as feminine and as something that gave or withheld great favours, and if she did wild or wicked things is was because she could not help them. The moon affects her as it does a woman, he thought.[4]

Within the sea are things that man both loves and hates. Santiago does not, as critics have suggested, love all things "both great and small," like the Ancient Mariner. He hates the poisonous and treacherous Portuguese men-of-war and loves the turtles for eating the dangerous creatures. There is thus a dualism of good and evil within the sea, just as the sea itself may give favors or do "wicked" things. The old man, with the patience of a Job, has usually accepted the fact that the sea can withhold its favors. He has had even longer runs of bad luck. But this time he purposely changes his patterns to change his luck. He isolates himself from the community of fishermen and journeys farther out than ever before.

As he travels out, a man-of-war bird appears. "The bird is a great help," the old man says, and he follows the course of the bird. The bird and a school of fish symbolically lead him over the edge of the world of men, across the threshold into the world of gods. After catching a tuna for bait, he continues until he hooks the marlin. He would like to avoid a battle, to have an easy victory, and he hopes that his catch will be easy to control.

But Santiago has been overanxious. The marlin has the hook in its mouth. When the hook sinks in, the marlin begins the long pull toward the northwest. The battle with the gods will not be an easy one. As the fish pulls, Santiago thinks of how the fish has chosen the direction because of Santiago's own treachery.

His choice had been to stay in the deep dark water far out beyond all snares and traps and treacheries. My choice was to go there to find him beyond all people. Beyond all people in the world. Now we are joined together and have been since noon. And no one to help either one of us.[5]

Santiago's choice was to extend himself beyond the human, and thus to extend human treachery out into the world of the gods. He has intentionally gone beyond the limits of mankind.

During the first night, another fish takes one of the baits, "a marlin or a broadbill or a shark," but Santiago cuts it loose. He deliberately chooses to follow the quest of the big fish rather than to sacrifice his opportunity for what might be an ordinary catch. The next day a small bird sits on the line and Santiago talks to it. He asks the bird if this is its first trip, and then does not warn the bird that hawks will be coming out to meet it. "Take a good rest, small bird," he says. "Then go in and take your chance like any man or bird or fish."[6] The bird, however, will be going in the opposite direction, the direction Santiago will take on his return to the world. This is not merely a foreshadowing of the danger that Santiago will face on his return trip; it is a statement of the condition of man. The bird is going into the world, where it will meet the type of dangers Santiago is familiar with.

Carlos Baker divides the chase into three stages: the time in which Santiago is unable to see his adversary, the continuation of the chase after the marlin appears, and the final circling action of the fish and Santiago's successful kill.[7] During the first two stages of the chase Santiago thinks about how lucky it is that the men do not have to kill the moon and the stars, and about his adversary, and about how he misses the boy. Finally, the crucial moment arrives, and Santiago is ready to bring the fish in for the kill. He is tired, his hands are "mush" and his vision is blurred. He tries to bring the fish in close, but fails repeatedly. Each time he feels himself "going" but always he thinks he will "try it once again." Finally, he brings the fish close.

He took all his pain and what was left of his strength and his long gone pride and he put it against the fish's agony and the fish came over onto his side and swam gently on his side, his bill almost touching the planking of the skiff and started to pass the boat, long, deep, wide, silver and barred with purple and interminable in the water.

The old man dropped the line and put his foot on it and lifted the harpoon as high as he could and drove it down with all his strength, and more strength he had just summoned, into the fish's side just behind the great chest fin that rose high in the air to the altitude of the man's chest. He felt the iron go in and he leaned on it and drove it further and then pushed all his weight after it.[8]

The fish makes its last surge and the sea is discolored with its blood. The old man, having called forth strength from beyond his physical nature, feels faint and sick.

The old man looked carefully in the glimpse of vision that he had. Then he took two turns of the harpoon line around the bitt in the bow and laid his head on his hands.[9]

He has had a visionary glimpse, and for a moment he pauses to rest. Rovit suggests that "this angling vision into the heart of mysteries cannot be brought back to the community of men." This is true in terms of Hemingway's presentation, of course. There is a choice for Santiago to make, however, in terms of the heroic adventure. Joseph Campbell states that the human responsibility of the return has often been refused. Many heroes have taken up residence forever in the "blessed isle of the unaging Goddess of Immortal Being."[10] But Santiago is not Melville's Ahab, motivated by a monomaniacal dream of vengeance. Santiago is a fisherman, and part of the reason for his quest has been to bring back food. His has been a purposeful quest in terms of his community. Santiago immediately recaptures his mortal senses. His sense of human duty and responsibility is too strong to allow him to regress into the bliss of the final cause. The work that he has generally thought of as a man's duty, however, he now thinks of as "slave work."

"Keep my head clear," he said against the wood of the bow. "I am a tired old man. But I have killed the fish which is my brother and now I must do the slave work."[11]

He refers to the slave work again a little later when he is forcing himself to the task.

"Get to work old man," he said. He took a very small drink of the water. "There is very much slave work to be done now that the fight is over."[12]

He accomplishes his work and begins to question the reality of the whole adventure. He remembers that more than once he had felt that there was some "great strangeness," that he had been in a dream. Even the fact that his hands and back are painful does not completely convince him of the reality of his adventure.

Then his head started to become a little unclear and he thought, is he bringing me in or am I bringing him in? If I were towing him behind there would be no question. Nor if the fish were in the skiff, with all dignity gone, there would be no question either.[13]

He keeps looking at the fish to make sure that the adventure in which he has been engaged has been a real one. The two of them, like brothers, start the return journey. They are going in the direction that the litle warbler bird had gone, and they must face all the perils. They are hit by sharks. The first is a Mako shark with as much beauty and dignity as the marlin. It has no fear and makes a direct attack. Santiago kills this shark with the harpoon. He has already begun to wish that he had not killed the marlin. "It might as well have been a dream, he thought. I cannot keep him from hitting me but maybe I can get him."[14] After the shark is dead Santiago begins to wish the killing of the fish had been a dream. Then he thinks,

"But man is not made for defeat," he said. "A man can be destroyed but not defeated." I am sorry that I killed the fish, though, he thought.[15]

He recognizes that there will be more sharks, and he has lost his harpoon in the big Mako. Between the time that he kills this shark and the attacks that come later, he has time to think about the morality of killing the great marlin. Twice he goes over essentially the same ground.

The pattern that leads him into thinking about sin begins with the return of hope.

It is silly not to hope, he thought. Besides, I believe it is a sin. Do not think about sin, he thought. There are enough problems now without sin. Also I have no understanding of it.[16]

But he continues to think about it. Then he thinks again about the killing of the fish, and once more he is conscious of sin.

Perhaps it was a sin to kill the fish. I suppose it was even though I did it to keep me alive and feed many people. But then everything is a sin.[17]

And after trying to quit thinking, he faces the question more honestly, admitting that he was motivated by pride.

. . . and he kept on thinking about sin. You did not kill the fish only to keep alive and to sell for food, he thought. You killed him for pride and because you are a fisherman. You loved him when he was alive and you loved him after. If you love him, it is not a sin to kill him. Or is it more?[18]

Santiago cannot resolve the question regarding sin, but he does learn the answer to his question about hope. As the great Mako shark comes in to destroy the fish, Santiago attacks. Hope is replaced by something else.

The old man's head was clear and good now and he was full of resolution but he had little hope.[19]

And when he hits the shark, he hits it "without hope but with resolution and complete malignancy."[20] His belief that man can be destroyed but not defeated is tested later. He has only defeated one shark, a shark that has approached directly with a dignity that the old man can respect. He has not met the treacherous sharks closer to shore that come in packs. They are a different breed of shark, *galanos*.

They were hateful sharks, bad smelling, scavengers as well as killers, and when they were hungry they would bite at an oar or the rudder of a boat. It was these sharks that would cut the turtles' legs and flippers off when the turtles were asleep on the surface, and they would hit a man in the water, if they were hungry, even if the man had no smell of fish blood nor of fish slime on him.[21]

These sharks are much like the Portuguese men-of-war. They are treacherous, and they are the beasts who complete the circle of good and evil relationships. These sharks eat the turtles who feed upon the treacherous Portuguese men-of-war. They are also different in that there is no dignity in their method of attack.

They came. But they did not come as the Mako had come. One turned and went out of sight under the skiff and the old man could feel the skiff shake as he jerked and pulled on the fish.[22]

But the old man continues to fight the treacherous sharks, killing them, too, with malignancy. He maintains his resolution, but he is becoming even more sorry that he has gone beyond "human limits" to seek out this fish. The sharks' treachery makes him more aware of his own treachery. He addresses the fish. He says aloud, "I wish it were a dream and that I had never hooked him. I'm sorry about it, fish. It makes everything wrong." He continues, "I shouldn't have gone out so far, fish, . . ." "Neither for you nor for me. I'm sorry, fish."[23] Throughout the day he battles the sharks. By dusk the marlin is half gone. Santiago is getting closer to the land. His proximity to the shore and safety makes him think quite differently about the human society that he had so willingly left behind him at the beginning of his quest.

I cannot be too far out now, he thought. I hope no one has been too worried. There is only the boy to worry, of course. But I am sure he would have confidence. Many of the other fishermen will worry. Many others too, he thought. I live in a good town.[24]

The emotional pull now is toward the community of men. He begins to feel alone, and to miss the boy. Then something with regard to the fish comes into his head, and he apologizes.

"Half fish," he said. 'Fish that you were. I am sorry that I went too far out. I ruined us both. But we have killed many sharks, you and I, and ruined many others."[25]

He thinks of the fish and the ability it would have to kill sharks if it were still alive. Then he thinks about how many sharks they could have killed had they been able to join forces—if Santiago had been able to cut off the marlin's bill and lash it to an oar butt. The man, however, did not have the proper tools, and god-fish and man could not join together in the battle against the sharks. There is no return of hope, but there is no diminution of his resolution. "I'll fight them until I die."[26] Again he recognizes that he has violated his "human" luck, and remembers that he tried to buy it at sea. He then comes to understand that he almost succeeded in his attempt with the gods. "They nearly sold it to you too," he thinks.[27]

Santiago's battle with the sharks on the return journey may be divided into three phases. First is his initial encounter with the Mako shark that makes a direct attack. Second is his gradually losing battle with the *galanos* during the day. In these battles, he loses all of the pointed weapons that are capable of killing the enemy. At the beginning of the return journey, he has hope for a successful return until he sights the first shark. This is replaced by resolution, although he knows that he will never get the marlin back to the land. As the third and final stage of the battle begins he has lost all hope for a successful return with his prize. As the darkness descends, he begins to hope again. This time, however, he does not hope for success; he hopes only that he will not have to fight again. But the gods do not give him any luck, and the sharks attack. There is nothing he can do but club the fish as they tear at the marlin's body. He fights until he uses up all weapons and there is no meat left on the carcass. He has continued to fight with resolution, even after he feels something break within him. His philosophy that man was not created for defeat is shattered. "He knew he was beaten now finally and without remedy,"[28] and he pays no attention to the sharks picking the bones of the carcass. As Lewis notes, "He must be completely humiliated before he can emerge from the sea as the new man."[29]

The battle has been lost, and his reaction is significant. There is no bitterness. He still believes that the forces of nature, the wind and the sea, may be his friends as well as his enemies. He recognizes how easy his progress is now that the battle is over and he has been beaten, and he is very much aware of what has defeated him. His answer to his own question about what has beaten him is "Nothing. I went out too far."[30] He has been beaten by his own treachery.

When he finally arrives at the harbor, he carries the mast back up the hill to his house and falls into bed. No one is there to help him beach the boat, and he carries the cross-like mast up the hill in silence and without thinking. He falls once, watches a cat that is going about its business at night with no knowledge of man's tragic struggles,[31] and then goes on. He must sit down to rest five times on his way. Only at the beginning of this climb does he turn to look at the skeleton. Joseph Campbell says that "the modern hero" must find his own way.

It is not society that is to guide and save the creative hero, but precisely the reverse. And so every one of us shares the supreme ordeal—carries the cross of the redeemer—not in the bright moments of his tribe's great victories, but in the silence of his personal despair.[32]

Santiago has carried his cross up the hill in the silence of his own despair. The skeleton of the fish, spiritual symbol of his victory, will be misunderstood by most of the world. The actual evidence of his battle and of the return is what affects the boy. Manolin, having already seen the skeleton of the fish, sees Santiago's hands and begins to cry. When he leaves to get coffee for the old man, he passes the fishermen who are measuring the skeleton. He does not express interest in their findings; he merely indicates his belief that it was an eighteen-foot fish. He does not care that they see him crying, and his only concern is that they do not disturb Santiago. Again, when he is complimented on his own catch as he orders the coffee, he begins to cry. The old man is asleep when Manolin returns with the coffee, and the boy waits patiently. In the first words Santiago speaks, he admits his defeat.

"Don't sit up," the boy said. "Drink this." He poured some of the coffee in a glass.

The old man took it and drank it.

"They beat me, Manolin," he said. "They truly beat me."[33]

There is ambiguity as well as a deliberate protective duplicity in Santiago's confession. Physically, the sharks beat him, but he explains it as though he is telling about the sharks as hostile and powerful forces beneath the sea. The indefinite "they" emphasizes the symbolic aspect of the treachery within the sea on the way home. Manolin makes a clear distinction.

"He didn't beat you. Not the fish."

"No. Truly. It was afterwards."[34]

Santiago makes it clear that he was not defeated in his quest against the gods. He informs the boy that it was only after his victory that he was defeated by the treacherous forces in the dualistic sea. But he does not mention the truth that he had found for himself—that he had gone out too far. He does not mention his own human treachery to the boy, although he hints at it when he tells Manolin that he is no longer lucky.

The boy asks what is to be done with the head and the spear, and Santiago wills the head to Pedrico and the spear to Manolin. The boy gladly accepts the symbol of maturity, and immediately begins to make plans. But Santiago must be assured first of his connection with mankind.

> "Did they search for me?" [he asks]
> "Of course. With coast guard and with planes."[35]

Then the old man excuses the failure of the searching parties.

> "The ocean is very big and a skiff is small and hard to see," the old man said. He noticed how pleasant it was to have someone to talk to instead of speaking only to himself and to the sea. "I missed you," he said. "What did you catch?"[36]

The boy tells him, indicating his successful fishing trips. At this point, however, it becomes clear that Manolin will supercede Santiago in following the role of the hero. He takes the adult role, breaking from his family and the authority of his father in order to go in the way of Santiago. It is Manolin who insists that they once more fish together.

"Now we fish together again."

"No. I am not lucky. I am not lucky anymore."

"The hell with luck," the boy said. "I'll bring the luck with me."[37]

The shift in allegiance has immediate results, and the old man once more begins to plan for another trip. In his planning, he includes the things that were missing on his last trip and which made it impossible for him to bring back the marlin. The boy orders him to get his hands well, and to heal that which was broken in his chest during the night battle. Finally, the boy questions him about the suffering. As Manolin leaves with the realization of the suffering, he is crying again. The boy's loyalty has been won not so much by the victory over the fish but through the boy's recognition of the suffering that Santiago has endured and his sympathy for the old man.

Santiago must at least unconsciously recognize the importance of the quest. Although he is willing to admit to Manolin that he has been defeated by the sharks, he gives the boy directions for equipping the boat for another trip in which Manolin is obviously going to lead. He does not, as he well might, warn the boy that he was beaten, as he has admitted to himself, because he went out too far. As in his refusal to warn the little bird flying to shore, he recognizes that Manolin too will have to find out for himself, will have to take his chance "like any man or bird or fish."

The fishermen who see the marlin's skeleton see in it only the representation of the biggest fish that has ever been caught in their knowledge. The tourists in the concluding ironic passage are unable even to recognize the type of fish, and in a sense confuse the very nature of good and evil and man's relation to it. With perhaps even greater irony, in the final paragraph of the novel, the old man lies in his bed dreaming of the young lion cubs playing on the beach. Santiago is the hero who has been out to touch the great secrets. He has killed the big fish and has felt its heart with his harpoon. But he has also learned that he can bring nothing home from the battle with the gods except a symbol of his victory, and that in the bringing home lies the great defeat. Nevertheless, his unconscious mind brings back the dreams of the happy shores and the young lions. As Emily Dickinson once put it in a very short poem:

> We lose—because we win—
> Gamblers—recollecting which
> Toss their dice again![38]

Fishermen, as Santiago well knows, are gamblers, as are all men. He has lost because he has won. Thus, there is an ambiguity even with regard to the defeat. Hemingway is reported to have told A. E. Hotchner,

"There is at the heart of it [The Old Man and the Sea] the oldest double dicho I know."
"What's a double dicho?" I asked.
"It's a saying that makes a statement forward or backward. Now this dicho is: Man can be destroyed but not defeated."
"Man can be defeated but not destroyed."
"Yes, that's its inversion, but I've always preferred to believe that man is undefeated."[39]

Whatever Hemingway's preference, he was enough of an artist to recreate the dualistic concept of the *dicho*. Santiago is defeated by his own treachery in going out too far and by the sharks as the agents on his return, but he has not been destroyed. He has endured throughout the quest, and the battle during the return. He spits blood into the ocean and says to the sharks, "Eat that, *Galanos*. And make a dream you've killed a man."[40]

Santiago has also been destroyed. He has lost hope, and the loss of hope he recognizes as the most grievous of sins. His pride, his ego, has been totally demolished in the battle with the sharks. After the battle is over, he thinks only of how "easy" it is now that he has been beaten. But he is not *totally* defeated, for he responds to the boy's faith and interest, and to the knowledge that he has been missed by the community. At the very last, he is dreaming the old dream about the lions on the beach. The ego is undergoing an unconscious regeneration as the old man sleeps.

The *double dicho* has been accomplished successfully through the final dream image, and that image also suggests the complexity of the work. The quest hero as saint has completed the cycle and the fable has been resolved. The narrator's descriptions of the hero have increased the fabular quality of the story, but Hemingway has also been careful to portray Santiago as a human being. This becomes especially clear in the final sentence, where the old man dreams of the lions. The humility that Santiago acquired through his defeat on the return is, perhaps, saintlike. But the unconscious remains human. As Robert W. Lewis points out through a quotation from M. C. D'Arcy's *The Mind and Heart of Love: Lion and Unicorn, a Study in Eros and Agape,* the lion frequently symbolizes both a noble and ignoble self-centered love, a love which involves pride, self-respect, and honor.[41] The lions, which Santiago saw in his youth, are also closely associated with the boy Manolin. Santiago dreams only of

places now and of the lions on the beach. They played like young cats in the dusk and he loved them as he loved the boy. He never dreamed about the boy.[42]

As Lewis notes, "the conscious mind would revolt at substituting Manolin in the dream, but the unconscious asserts the relationship."[43] It is also significant that the narrator's description of the old man's dream the morning before he begins his quest indicates what the old man does *not* dream. His dreams are no longer concerned with worldly self-centered pride in the most obvious sense. But the importance of the final dream and its association with Manolin bears further analysis.

Although the quest and the return provide the most important conflicts within the novel, it is also important to understand the basic motivation that leads Santiago to begin the quest. Manolin has been fishing with Santiago since he was a child of five. Santiago has, in a sense, been the boy's spiritual father. But because the old man has had no luck, the boy's parents insist that Manolin fish with the more practical fishermen. The parents represent a countering influence, the influence of the community rather than its heroes or leaders. As Rovit suggests

As they must, most men spend the greatest part of their lives enwrapped in a world where prudence and practicality are the measurements of what is. Living within the blanketing hum of everyday reality with solid earth beneath their feet, men cannot see what they have no eyes for, nor can they understand what they have not been prepared to understand.[44]

With his own pride in his way of life, Santiago has been tutoring the boy, but is now losing his influence over him. As he tells Manolin, "If you were my boy I'd take you out and gamble. But you are your father's and your mother's and you are in a lucky boat."[45] There is, then, a conflict between Santiago and the boy's parents for control of the life of the boy, and it is partly because of the boy that Santiago goes out to sea.

From a very simplified application of Freudian psychological symbolism, the relationship between the old man and the boy might be seen as an attachment with homosexual overtones. From the viewpoint of Adler's psychology of power, the emphasis would be shifted to the struggle for dominance in controlling the life of Manolin. But in the quest-hero context, the emphasis is upon the quest for immortality through the influence of Santiago upon the new generation. From any viewpoint, Santiago wins the contest. At the end of the novel, the parents and the limited vision they represent have been defeated. The torture of Santiago has resulted in the deliverance of Manolin from the authority of his parents. Santiago's Christ-like, or saintly, function, to "set a man at variance against his father" (Matthew, X, 35) has been accomplished. Manolin is now truly a disciple of Santiago. He is anxious to return to the sea with the old man, to learn everything he can from him. Santiago's spiritual ego has found its home in the ego of another.

Santiago's motivations have been saintly, but sinfully human as well. The result of his ordeal has been the re-creation of his own heroic ego in Manolin. He has achieved this victory through suffering. What he has achieved for himself is also significant. Santiago is too complex to appear as the typically pure fabular hero. He has restored his own ego through the quest and its influence; though he has conducted himself as a saint, his motivations have been those of human pride.

Though the boon that Santiago has brought home has been only a symbolic one which is misinterpreted by almost all who see it, he has learned much from his journey. He has lost the pride that has given him a feeling of superiority. He has learned to miss his fellow men, and it is not incidental that, just before Manolin leaves, Santiago cautions the boy not to forget to give the head to Pedrico.

Perhaps another appropriate poem by Emily Dickinson may serve to emphasize the contrast between Jason's quest of the Golden Fleece and Hemingway's adaptation of the myth to an old fisherman and his adventures. For there is a distinct difference in the stories.

> *Finding is the first Act*
> *The second, loss,*
> *Third, Expedition for*
> *The "Golden Fleece"*
>
> *Fourth, no Discovery —*
> *Fifth, no Crew —*
> *Finally, no Golden Fleece —*
> *Jason — sham — too.*[46]

Once again the concept of loss is evident, and the quest is suggested as a meaningless and self-destructive venture. Most important, the suggestion that there are no pure heroes emphasizes the irony of the baseball conversations early in the novel. It is not through the inspirational victories of the Joe DiMaggios that the true heroism is displayed and that the "heroic" character of mankind can be formed; it is through the recognition of man's ultimate defeat, which he endures with resolution and courage and which brings him into an acceptance of reality, that a conditional victory is won.

Although Sheridan Baker is certainly correct when he suggests that Hemingway returns in this novel to the "Winner Take Nothing" posture of the early stories,[47] it should be noted that there is still an ambiguity in *The Old Man and the Sea* that is not evident in such stories as "The Undefeated." As a parable, *The Old Man and the Sea* contains both elements of the "double *dicho*," and it responds well to a pessimistic as well as an optimistic interpretation. More specifically than "coming full-circle," Hemingway has arrived at a fusion of his earlier naturalistic and later romantic positions in his treatment of the hero in this final effort. This fusion is largely a result of Hemingway's acceptance of life, as Sheridan Baker well understands. The early anti-heroes and their ineffective humanity in the face of an amoral and powerful universe are mirrored in Santiago's defeat by the powers of the sharks. The romantic heroes of *For Whom the Bell Tolls* and *Across the River and Into the Trees* can be seen in Santiago's battles with the marlin. But another quality of resignation and resolution has been added to the role that the unheroic hero must play in a dualistic universe. Santiago is a complex saint-like but sinful and very human hero, and his is the last face of the hero that Hemingway would portray.

CONCLUSION

IN ERNEST HEMINGWAY's purported answer to A. E. Hotchner's question with regard to the "recurring hero"—"Does Yogi Berra have a grooved swing?"—it is apparent that Hemingway did not himself think that he had been writing about what has been called a "progressive" hero. Yogi Berra was, for many years, one of the most dangerous hitters in baseball, and he was feared by opposing pitchers primarily because he would hit anything, high, low, middle, inside, outside. He did not have what is called a "grooved swing." Yet until recently, much of Hemingway criticism has been based on the concept of the recurring or progressive hero. For the most part, Hemingway criticism has been exceptionally good, and what has appeared in print will continue to serve as a firm basis upon which other critics may work.

But the progresive hero concept, though continually being modified, is also restrictive at times, especially when the hero is too closely tied to the life of the man Ernest Hemingway and the legend he helped to create. What I have tried to demonstrate is that, taken as separate works of art, the Hemingway novels are quite different in conception and technique and that the protagonists are distinctly different characters. Though they may have their similarities, they are fictional creations that exist within specific contexts. What becomes apparent after separate examinations of each of the novels is that Hemingway seems to have shifted directions rather drastically in his career as novelist—in ideology, in sensibility, and in technique. And this becomes especially clear in his treatment of the protagonists of the novels.

In the first four novels, the protagonists do not function as heroes at all. They are essentially anti-heroes in a naturalistic reaction to the hero concept. The first novel, *The Torrents of Spring*, is in fact a satiric attack against the contemporary sentimental "heroes" of Sherwood Anderson's novels. What Hemingway seems to suggest is "a plague on heroes," especially as the hero appears in two of Anderson's novels, *Many Marriages* and *Dark Laughter*. In Hemingway's next two novels, the protagonists are unheroic, but in different ways. Jake Barnes is the physically wounded protagonist who learns that he must face the world with resignation, and he learns part of this lesson from the traditional heroic type, the Romero-Belmonte figure. The protagonist of *A Farewell to Arms* is wounded psychologically, not only by the chaotic war-torn world around him, but by his own failures and guilt. His failure is sharply contrasted to the self-sacrifice of the heroine Catherine Barkley. Harry Morgan of *To Have and Have Not* is a convincingly drawn anti-hero, and the last in Hemingway's treatment of the unheroic protagonist. There are no heroes in *To Have and Have Not*, the only one of Hemingway's novels to be set in the United States.

In these early works, Hemingway had worked well

within the naturalistic framework and with a naturalistic sensibility, concentrating largely on his tragic view of the life of man in a deterministic world. Something changed, however, and the novel that grew out of his personal involvement in the Spanish Civil War is a very different novel. *For Whom the Bell Tolls* is his first novel to have a heroic protagonist. Here Hemingway presented a prototype of the mythic warrior hero in a contemporary setting. More important than any change in his political views is the change in his artistic sensibility which can be seen not only in his technique but in the role that he gives his hero Robert Jordan. His final two novels demonstrate two different faces of the hero; the protagonist of *Across the River and Into the Trees* is Colonel Cantwell, the tyrant hero, and Santiago of *The Old Man and the Sea* is the sinning hero as saint. Each is a hero, but a different version of the hero.

Hemingway's talent was a large talent, and his growth as writer and artist is evident in an examination of the novels. Not content to continue in the method and with the same concepts of his early successes, he moved in his concept of the hero from showing man as he was in this world to an examination of what man could be. And in the writing, he experimented with techniques he had not used before, trying to make what he wrote valid not merely for this year but for ten years and perhaps for always. He fished sometimes too far out; sometimes his reach exceeded his grasp. But few writers have faced the dangers of fishing in the seas he fished, and even fewer brought home any bigger catch. He left us a montage of faces of the hero—man and his potential.

NOTES

Introduction

1. A. E. Hotchner, *Papa Hemingway* (New York, 1966), p. 180. Hemingway purportedly said this in a conversation with Hotchner.

2. Granville Hicks, *The Great Tradition: An Interpretation of American Literature Since the Civil War* (New York, 1935), pp. 273-274.

3. *Ibid.,* p. 274.

4. George Snell, *The Shapers of American Fiction, 1798-1947* (New York, 1947), p. 149.

5. Philip Young, *Ernest Hemingway* (New York, 1952), p. 38.

6. Ernest Hemingway, *Death in the Afternoon* (New York, 1934), p. 91.

7. Princeton, New Jersey, 1956.

8. New York, 1965.

9. Earl Rovit, *Ernest Hemingway* (New Haven, Conn., 1963). Philip Young calls Rovit's book the "best full-length Hemingway book since Fenton's" in his article, "Our Hemingway Man," *Kenyon Review,* XXVI, No. 4 (Autumn 1965), 691.

10. *Ibid.,* p. 55.

11. Robert W. Lewis, Jr., *Hemingway on Love* (Austin, Texas, 1965). See, for example, his warning to the reader, "Obviously those critics who read this pair of short stories as autobiographical do so at their own considerable risk. Such exercises as Philip Young and Carlos Baker perform in drawing parallels are suggestive and stimulating but still hazardous" (p. 79).

12. Two books have appeared too recently to be included in the text of this study: Leo Gurko's *Ernest Hemingway and the Pursuit of Heroism* and Jackson J. Benson's *Hemingway: The Writer's Art of Self-Defense.* Benson's work is another extremely important critical analysis of Hemingway's art, ranking with Rovit and Lewis in insights. Professor Benson's analysis of the narrative perspective

in *The Old Man and the Sea* precisely identifies the major problem of Hemingway's last novel.

chapter 1

1. Carlos Baker *(Hemingway: The Writer as Artist)* says, "The book was written with astonishing speed and great concentration during a little more than seven days in November, 1925" (p. 37).

2. For a discussion of the publishing history, see Carlos Baker, pp. 37-38; Arthur Mizener, *The Far Side of Paradise* (Boston, 1949), pp. 196-197; and Andrᵉw Turnbull, ed., *The Letters of F. Scott Fitzgerald* (New York, 1963), pp. 195-198.

3. 1250 copies of *The Torrents of Spring* were printed for the first edition. *The Sun Also Rises,* published approximately five months later, had a first edition of 5090 copies. See Lee D. Samuels, *A Hemingway Check-List* (New York, 1951), p. 10.

4. Carlos Baker, p. 38.

5. See Carlos Baker's discussion, pp. 40-42.

6. Turnbull, p. 195. The passage has been quoted by Mizener, Baker, and others, but without reference to a later statement in the same letter that "He's anxious too to get a foot-hold in your magazine. . . ." and, from a later letter, "To hear him talk you'd think Liveright had broken up his home and robbed him of millions—but that's because he knows nothing of publishing, except in the cuckoo magazines, is very young and feels helpless so far away" (pp. 197-198).

7. Sherwood Anderson, *Dark Laughter* (New York, 1925), p. 310.

8. Carlos Baker says that the writing of *The Torrents of Spring* "came as a kind of interlude of 'relaxation' between the completion of the first draft of *The Sun Also Rises* and the beginning of the final rewriting job" (pp. 37-38).

9. Hemingway's letter to Fitzgerald concerning his revision of *The Sun Also Rises* shows the importance of Cohn as a character. He

wrote, "I cut The Sun to start with Cohn—cut all that first part."
See Mizener, *The Far Side of Paradise*, p. 198.

10. Ernest Hemingway, *The Torrents of Spring* (New York, 1939),
pp. 123-124.

11. *Ibid.*, pp. 93-94.

12. Sherwood Anderson, *Many Marriages* (New York, 1923), pp.
255-256.

13. *Dark Laughter*, p. 90.

14. *The Torrents of Spring*, pp. 19-20.

15. *Dark Laughter*, p. 17.

16. *The Torrents of Spring*, pp. 4-5.

17. Carlos Baker sees the "shade of D. H. Lawrence" in the bird
scenes, and this is certainly a satire on Lawrence, as well as on Anderson's adaptation of Lawrence's use of symbolism.

18. *The Torrents of Spring*, pp. 12-13.

19. *Ibid.*, pp. 20-21.

20. *Ibid.*, p. 22.

21. *Ibid.*, p. 55.

22. *Ibid.*, p. 133.

23. Lewis, p. 6.

24. *Dark Laughter*, p. 230.

25. *The Torrents of Spring*, p. 55.

26. *Ibid.*, p. 51.

27. *Ibid.*, p. 138.

28. *Ibid.*, p. 141.

29. *Ibid.*, p. 5.

30. *Ibid.*, p. 69.

31. *Ibid.*, pp. 74-75.

32. *Ibid.*, p. 14.

33. *Ibid.*, p. 85.

34. *Ibid.*, p. 89.

35. Philip Young, *Ernest Hemingway* (New York, 1952), p. 233.

chapter II

1. A. E. Hotchner, *Papa Hemingway*, p. 51.

2. Part of the reason for this, of course, was Hemingway's use of the Gertrude Stein quotation "You are all a lost generation." The assumption was, and sometimes still is, that Jake Barnes is part of the "all." Henry Seidel Canby (*American Memoir* [Boston, 1947]) says that *The Sun Also Rises* "reflected the life of psychological derelicts floating in alcohol and tormented by oversensitive nerves. Yet these derelicts, expatriated in Paris, were evidently symbolic of a change in values, more easily seen in these neurotics than in better-balanced youngsters of the new generation at home" (p. 339).

3. Ernest Hemingway, *The Sun Also Rises* (New York, 1926), p. 36. All page references are to The Scribner Library Edition, SL 5.

4. Andrew Turnbull, ed., *The Letters of F. Scott Fitzgerald*, p. 205.

5. Actually he is from the Midwest, but is representative of a more conservative environment.

6. Note that in "The Killers," for example, Nick Adams does not want to think about what has happened in the cafe. He cannot help thinking about it in the sense of remembering it, but he does not want to think about the implications.

7. *The Sun Also Rises*, p. 148.

8. Henry David Thoreau, *Walden,* ed., Sherman Paul (Boston, 1957), p. 62.

9. *The Sun Also Rises*, p. 148.

10. See William James, *Essays in Pragmatism*, ed., Alburey Castell (New York, 1961).

11. *The Sun Also Rises*, p. 149.

12. Ernest Hemingway, *Death in the Afternoon* (New York, 1932), p. 4.

13. This discussion of Jake's moral position is limited to Jake's statements and actions within the novel. For an excellent discussion of Hemingway's concept of morality and immorality, see Max Westbrook, "The Stewardship of Ernest Hemingway," *The Texas Quarterly* (Winter, 1966), pp. 89-101.

14. *The Sun Also Rises,* p. 149.
15. *Ibid.,* p. 130.
16. *Ibid.*
17. *Ibid.,* p. 233.
18. *Ibid.,* p. 61.
19. *Ibid.,* p. 65.
20. *Ibid.,* p. 72.
21. *Ibid.,* p. 53.
22. *Ibid.,* p. 52.
23. *Ibid.,* p. 106.
24. *Ibid.,* p. 76.
25. *Ibid.,* p. 156.
26. *Ibid.,* pp. 109-110.
27. *Ibid.,* p. 132.
28. *Ibid.*
29. *Ibid.,* p. 236.
30. *Ibid.*
31. *Ibid.*
32. *Ibid.,* p. 77.
33. *Ibid.,* p. 96.
34. *Ibid.,* p. 97.
35. *Ibid.,* p. 232.
36. See Earl Rovit, *Ernest Hemingway,* pp. 152ff.
37. Mark Spilka, "The Death of Love in *The Sun Also Rises,*" in Carlos Baker, ed., *Ernest Hemingway: Critiques of Four Major Novels* (New York, 1962), pp. 18-25.
38. *The Sun Also Rises,* p. 37. Note Macomber's selection of a drink and the reason for it. "I suppose it's the thing to do," . . . "Tell him to make three gimlets." (*The Short Stories of Ernest Hemingway* [1953], p. 3.)
39. *Ibid.,* p. 107.
40. *Ibid.,* p. 31.

41 *Ibid.*, p. 182.

42. *Ibid.*, p. 191.

43. *Ibid.*, p. 194.

44. *Ibid.*, pp. 214-215.

45. In this sense, Jake would be making an attempt to destroy Brett's illusion that she is capable of love. Brett is obviously the "new" woman. She wears a man's hat and is accepted easily by the homosexuals at the beginning of the novel. Jake must feel that she will be forced into a traditional female role by the extremely masculine Romero. The confusion of sexual roles in France is quite evident in the novel.

46. *The Sun Also Rises*, p. 35.

47. *Ibid.*, p. 184.

48. See Lord Raglan, *The Hero* (New York, 1956), p. 150, for a description of the characteristics of the typical ritual pattern.

49. Robert W. Lewis, *Hemingway on Love*, p. 34.

50. An interesting approach for an analysis of the relationship of Jake to Lady Brett would be the use of Berne's *Games People Play* (New York, 1964). Jake Barnes plays "Wooden Leg," and Brett plays "Let's You and Him Fight" through much of the novel.

51. *The Sun Also Rises*, p. 239.

52. *Ibid.*, pp. 24-25.

53. *Ibid.*, p. 247.

Chapter III

1. For example, Carlos Baker *(Hemingway: The Writer as Artist)* says that "Malcolm Cowley has well described him as one of 'the haunted and nocturnal writers,' akin, in his deeper reaches, to Melville and Hawthorne" (p. 132). Cowley's highly important article appears as the introduction to *The Portable Hemingway* (New York, 1944).

2. George Snell, *The Shapers of American Fiction, 1798-1947*, p. 163.

3. Sheridan Baker, *Ernest Hemingway* (New York, 1967), p. 68. Baker says, "Catherine of the long blond hair, which first catches Henry's eye, which tents their kisses in bed, is not so womanly as Hemingway seems to suppose. She is uncomfortably similar to the sleek British Brett of Jake's hospital tour." Baker notes some comparisons of the two women made by Philip Young and adds a few of his own. However, it seems to me that he misses the point of Catherine's basic femininity.

4. J. D. Salinger, *The Catcher in the Rye* (Boston, 1951), pp. 182-183.

5. Ernest Hemingway, *A Farewell to Arms* (New York, 1929), p. 116. All page references are to The Scribner Library Edition, SL 61.

6. *Ibid.*, p. 299.

7. Carlos Baker, *Ernest Hemingway: Critiques of Four Major Novels*, p. 75.

8. *Ibid.*

9. *Ibid.*

10. *A Farewell to Arms*, p. 259.

11. Maurice Z. Shroder, "The Novel as Genre," in Philip Stevick (ed.), *The Theory of the Novel* (New York, 1967), p. 24. Originally published in *The Massachusetts Review*, 1963.

12. *A Farewell to Arms*, p. 206.

13. *Ibid.*, pp. 210-211.

14. *Ibid.*, p. 209.

15. E. M. Halliday, "Hemingway's Ambiguity: Symbolism and Irony," *American Literature*, XXVIII (March, 1956), 17. The article is reprinted in Baker's *Ernest Hemingway: Critiques of Four Major Novels*, pp. 61-74.

16. *A Farewell to Arms*, p. 212.

17. *Ibid.*, p. 233.

18. *Ibid.*, p. 241.

19. *Ibid.*, p. 39.

20. *Ibid.*, p. 240.

21. *Ibid.*, pp. 240-241.

22. *Ibid.*, p. 14.

23. *Ibid.*, p. 74.

24. *Ibid.*, p. 75.

25. John Killinger, *Hemingway and the Dead Gods: A Study in Existentialism* (New York, 1965), p. 61.

26. Note that a distinction is made in the reactions to the different types of joke (see pp. 8-9). The captain explains that when one goes away on leave, one goes in a manner represented by the thumb. When one returns, he comes back like the little finger. The reaction is, "Every one laughed." Then the captain repeats the joke, counting off the fingers. Frederic reports, "They all laughed." When the captain makes the reference to masturbation, Frederic Henry again reports that "*They* all laughed again" (my emphasis).

27. *A Farewell to Arms*, p. 67.

28. *Ibid.*, p. 176.

29. *Ibid.*, p. 13.

30. See James F. Light, "The Religion of Death in *A Farewell to Arms*," *Modern Fiction Studies*, VII (Summer, 1961), 169-173. It has been reprinted in Baker's *Ernest Hemingway: Critiques of Four Major Novels*, pp. 37-40.

31. *A Farewell to Arms*, p. 294.

32. *Ibid.*, p. 338.

33. *Ibid.*, p. 342.

34. Killinger, pp. 47-48.

35. *A Farewell to Arms*, pp. 258-259. This description is in an analysis of Catherine.

36. *Ibid.*, pp. 300-301.

37. *Ibid.*, p. 301.

38. *Ibid.*, p. 309.

39. *Ibid.*, p. 260.

40. *Ibid.*, p. 318.

41. *Ibid.*, p. 340.

42. Malcolm Cowley, Introduction to *The Portable Hemingway*, p. viii.

43. *A Farewell to Arms*, pp. 338-339.

44. *Ibid.*, p. 320.

45. *Ibid.*, p. 338.

46. Carlos Baker, *Ernest Hemingway: Critiques of Four Major Novels*, p. 75.

Chapter IV

1. Oscar Cargill, *Intellectual America* (New York, 1941), p. 363.

2. George Snell, *The Shapers of American Fiction*, p. 165.

3. W. M. Frohock, *The Novel of Violence in America, 1920-1950* (Dallas, 1950), p. 154.

4. Carlos Baker, *Hemingway: The Writer as Artist*, p. 205.

5. Sheridan Baker, *Ernest Hemingway*, p. 103.

6. Carlos Baker, p. 211.

7. Robert W. Lewis, Jr., *Hemingway on Love*, p. 117.

8. Ernest Hemingway, *To Have and Have Not* (New York, 1937), pp. 95-96. Evidently, Harry is right when he says that there "ain't much money in any kind of chances now," because he finally agrees to pay Albert $5 per day, just one dollar more per day than he had been paying the rummy Eddy for fishing.

9. Cargill, pp. 365-366.

10. Throughout the novel, Harry has had a tendency to blame others for his own failures. He even blames some sort of "fate" for his disappointment in his own daughters. He does not stop to think that he might be partly to blame. He is unable to see the relationship of the past to the present.

11. *To Have and Have Not*, p. 105.

12. *Ibid.*, p. 86.

13. *Ibid.*, p. 133. This remark is made to Bee-lips when Bee-lips warns Harry not to tell Freddy the details about the trip. The completely untrustworthy Bee-lips says that he wouldn't trust anybody. Harry replies, "*You* shouldn't. Not after the experiences you've had with yourself." Harry does not, finally, tell Freddy about the trip.

14. Carlos Baker, p. 210.

15. See Ray Allen Billington, *The Far Western Frontier 1830-1860* (New York, 1956), p. 49.

16. *To Have and Have Not*, p. 234.

17. Sheridan Baker, p. 104.

18. *To Have and Have Not*, p. 258.

19. Carlos Baker, pp. 215-216.

20. *To Have and Have Not*, p. 27.

21. See p. 85. Harry is so concerned about making a financially successful venture that he takes unnecessary chances in order to save the cargo.

22. *Ibid.*, p. 173.

23. *Ibid.*, p. 174.

24. Philip Young, *Ernest Hemingway*, p. 72.

25. John Killinger, *Hemingway and the Dead Gods*, p. 84.

26. Carlos Baker, pp. 204-205.

27. *To Have and Have Not*, p. 197.

28. *Ibid.*, p. 221.

29. *Ibid.*, p. 255.

30. Sheridan Baker sees Gordon's view of Marie Morgan as "one of Hemingway's subtlest effects." He admits that Delmore Schwartz found it "the worst moment in a bad book" (pp. 105-106). Strangely enough, Baker's treatment of the passage is not very perceptive, and why he considers it effective is never quite clear.

31. *To Have and Have Not*, p. 64.

32. Lewis, p. 139.

33. E. M. Halliday, "Hemingway's Narrative Perspective," *Sewanee Review*, LX (Spring, 1952), 212. The essay is reprinted in Carlos Baker's *Ernest Hemingway: Critiques of Four Major Novels*, pp. 174-182.

34. *To Have and Have Not*, p. 98.

35. *Ibid.*, p. 108.

36. *Ibid.*, p. 110.

37. *Ibid.*, p. 118.

38. *Ibid.*, p. 120.

39. *Ibid.*, p. 232.

40. *Ibid.*, p. 239.

41. *Ibid.*, p. 246.

42. Sheridan Baker, p. 104.

43. *To Have and Have Not*, p. 225.

44. *Ibid.*, pp. 180-181.

45. See C. G. Jung, *The Psychology of the Unconscious* (New York, 1947), pp. 402-427 in the chapter on "The Dual Mother Role." On pages 413 and 414, Jung describes the reactions of two patients: "Another patient had the following dream during a relapse, in which the libido was again wholly introverted for a time: 'She was entirely filled within by a great snake; only one end of the tail peeped out from her arm. She wanted to seize it, but it escaped her.' A patient with a very strong introversion (catatonic state) complained to me that a snake was stuck in her throat."

46. *To Have and Have Not*, p. 181.

47. Perhaps the best case I have heard made in defense of the novel and in justification for the lack of an effective central character was in a discussion with Edith Wylder. Her case was based on Hemingway's artistic integrity and the awareness that Hemingway had continued to defend the novel. This is Hemingway's only novel set in materialistic America. In an essentially materialistic culture, the argument was presented, there can be no hero, nor can there be a unified form in the novel. The last clause is also a point made by Robert Lewis, "Thus the form of the novel is a complementary series of degenerations and of episodes of growing violence" (p. 117).

chapter V

1. Joseph Campbell, *The Hero with a Thousand Faces* (New York, 1956), p. 388.

2. See Earl Rovit, *Ernest Hemingway*, pp. 140-141. Of special importance is the background material for his assertions on these two pages included in Section I of the chapter "Of Time and Style," pp. 126-136.

3. Carlos Baker, *Ernest Hemingway: The Writer as Artist*, p. 250.

4. Ernest Hemingway, *Death in the Afternoon*, p. 192.

5. Frederic J. Hoffman and Olga Vickery, *William Faulkner: Two Decades of Criticism* (East Lansing, Michigan, 1951), p. 119.

6. E. M. Halliday, "Hemingway's Narrative Perspective," p. 216.

7. Cowley links Hemingway with Hawthorne and Melville.

8. Jean-Paul Sartre, *Nausea* (New York, 1964), pp. 171-172.

9. John Killinger, *Hemingway and the Dead Gods*, p. 54.

10. Campbell, pp. 245-246. See also Lord Raglan, *The Hero: A Study in Tradition, Myth, and Drama* (New York, 1956), pp. 173-185. Jordan scores eleven points (possibly more) according to Lord Raglan's system of evaluation, and equalling Siegfried's total score. Lord Raglan states that historical heroes seldom score over six points, and it is significant, I think, that Jordan fails to earn points only in the category related to the mysterious birth and childhood of the mythical hero.

11. Erich Fromm, "The Present Human Condition," *The American Scholar*, XXV (Winter, 1955-56), 29-35. The quotation was taken from Louis G. Locke, William M. Gibson and George Arms, *Toward Liberal Education* (New York, 1967) 5th edition, p. 735.

12. Rovit, p. 136.

13. Ernest Hemingway, *For Whom the Bell Tolls* (New York, 1940), p. 4. All page references are to The Scribner Library Edition, SL 4.

14. *Ibid.*

15. *Ibid.*, p. 43.

16. *Ibid.*

17. *Ibid.*, p. 21.

18. *Ibid.*, p. 15. Jordan replies that he has not given any orders. Pablo is very much aware of Jordan's role, and answers, "You will though. There. There is the badness."

19. *Ibid.*, p. 239.

20. *Ibid.*, p. 456.

21. *Ibid.*, p. 175.

22. *Ibid.*, p. 404.

23. W. M. Frohock, *The Novel of Violence in America*, p. 198.

24. Robert W. Lewis, *Hemingway on Love*, p. 168.

25. Joseph Campbell, *The Masks of God: Primitive Mythology* (New York, 1959), p. 252.

26. Irving A. Hallowell, *The Role of Conjuring in Salteaux Society* (Philadelphia, 1952), p. 19.

27. *Hamlet*, Act III, Scene 1.

28. S. L. Frank, ed., *A Solovyov Anthology*, translated by Natalie Dunnington from the works of Vladimar S. Soloviev (New York, 1950), p. 162.

29. S. F. Sanderson, *Ernest Hemingway* (New York, 1961), p. 95.

30. Campbell, *The Hero with a Thousand Faces*, pp. 110-111.

31. *For Whom the Bell Tolls*, p. 161.

32. *Ibid.*, p. 159.

33. *Ibid.*, p. 379.

34. *Ibid.*

35. *Ibid.*, p. 467.

36. Campbell, *The Hero with a Thousands Faces*, p. 342.

37. *For Whom the Bell Tolls*, p. 212.

38. *Ibid.*, pp. 405-406. Note, too, that Jordan carefully avoids emotionality when saying goodbye to Anselmo (p. 410).

39. *Ibid.*, p. 461.

40. *Ibid.*, p. 462.

41. Campbell, *The Hero with a Thousand Faces*, p. 111.

42. *For Whom the Bell Tolls*, p. 391.

43. Rovit, p. 76.

44. *For Whom the Bell Tolls*, p. 464.

45. *Ibid.*, p. 70.

46. *Ibid.*, pp. 469-470.

47. *Ibid.*, p. 470.

48. Snell, *The Shapers of American Fiction*, p. 167.

Chapter VI

1. Almost all the reviews were negative. My own feelings at the time are embarrassingly recorded in a short review in *Western Review*, 15:3 (Spring, 1951), 237-240.

2. Young calls it a "failure," and "among his weakest [books]." See his discussion in his *Ernest Hemingway*, pp. 86-93.

3. Carlos Baker, *Ernest Hemingway: The Writer as Artist*, p. 265.

4. Young, p. 90.

5. John Killinger, *Hemingway and the Dead Gods*, p. 98.

6. A. E. Hotchner, *Papa Hemingway*, p. 202.

7. *The Sun Also Rises*, pp. 214-215.

8. Joseph Campbell, *The Hero with a Thousand Faces*, p. 353.

9. See Earl Rovit, *Ernest Hemingway*, p. 55ff.

10. Campbell, p. 337.

11. Ernest Hemingway, *Across the River and Into the Trees* (New York, 1950), p. 36.

12. *Ibid.*

13. *Ibid.*, p. 193.

14. *Ibid.*

15. *Ibid.*, p. 8.

16. *Ibid.*, pp. 92-93.

17. *Ibid.*, p. 289.

18. *Ibid.*, p. 87.

19. Young, p. 90.

20. *Across the River and Into the Trees*, p. 229.

21. *Ibid.*, p. 197.

22. *Ibid.*, p. 198.

23. *Ibid.*, p. 59. Note also the way he describes his own regiment, pp. 248-251.

24. *Ibid.*, p. 177.

25. Henry David Thoreau, *Walden*, p. 60. "Morning is when I am awake and there is a dawn in me."

26. *Across the River and Into the Trees*, p. 9.

27. *Ibid.*, p. 11.

28. *Ibid.*

29. *Ibid.*, p. 232.

30. *Ibid.*, p. 258.

31. *Ibid.*, p. 110.

32. *Ibid.*

33. *Ibid.*, p. 93.

34. *Ibid.*, p. 130.

35. *Ibid.*, pp. 131-132.

36. *Ibid.*, p. 199.

37. *Ibid.*, p. 301.

38. *Ibid.*, p. 302. Note the comparison in this scene to *A Farewell to Arms*, pp. 94-95.

39. *Ibid.*, p. 304.

40. *Ibid.*, p. 306.

41. Lord Raglan, *The Hero: A Study in Tradition, Myth, and Drama*, p. 190. This is a description of the traditional hero figure

who always fights alone, as contrasted to the historic figure who has an army or a retinue of followers.

42. *Across the River and Into the Trees,* p. 192.

43. *Ibid.,* p. 288.

44. Lord Raglan, pp. 193-194.

Chapter VII

1. Joseph Campbell, *The Hero with a Thousand Faces.* For a full discussion of this type of hero, see pp. 334-356.

2. *Ibid.,* p. 354.

3. Earl Rovit, *Ernest Hemingway,* p. 90.

4. Ernest Hemingway, *The Old Man and the Sea* (New York, 1952), pp. 32-33.

5. *Ibid.,* p. 55.

6. *Ibid.,* p. 61.

7. See *Ernest Hemingway: The Writer as Artist,* pp. 296-299.

8. *The Old Man and the Sea,* pp. 103-104.

9. *Ibid.,* pp. 104-105.

10. Campbell, p. 193. The "refusal of the return" is an important concept to be remembered in terms of quest literature. The great quest of Captain Ahab for Moby Dick ends in a note of ambiguity on this score as well as others. Has Ahab been joined to Moby Dick by a symbolic umbilical cord and carried to the world of the Gods, or is he merely drowned? The former interpretation would certainly justify Melville's statement to Hawthorne that he had written a "wicked" book.

11. *The Old Man and the Sea,* p. 105.

12. *Ibid.,* p. 106.

13. *Ibid.,* p. 109.

14. *Ibid.,* p. 112.

15. *Ibid.,* p. 114.

16. *Ibid.*, p. 115.

17. *Ibid.*, p. 116.

18. *Ibid.*

19. *Ibid.*, p. 112.

20. *Ibid.*, p. 113.

21. *Ibid.*, p. 119.

22. *Ibid.*

23. *Ibid.*, p. 121.

24. *Ibid.*, p. 127.

25. *Ibid.*

26. *Ibid.*, p. 128.

27. *Ibid.*, p. 129.

28. *Ibid.*, p. 131.

29. Robert W. Lewis, *Hemingway on Love*, p. 211.

30. *The Old Man and the Sea*, p. 133.

31. *Ibid.*, p. 134. See Carlos Baker, *Ernest Hemingway: The Writer as Artist*, pp. 319-320, for an excellent commentary on this scene.

32. Campbell, p. 391.

33. *The Old Man and the Sea*, p. 136.

34. *Ibid.*, pp. 136-137.

35. *Ibid.*, p. 137.

36. *Ibid.*

37. *Ibid.*

38. Thomas H. Johnson, ed., *The Poems of Emily Dickinson* (Cambridge, Mass., 1958), I, 22. I am greatly indebted to my wife, Edith P. Wylder, for calling this and the following Dickinson poem to my attention.

39. A. E. Hotchner, *Papa Hemingway*, p. 73.

40. *The Old Man and the Sea*, p. 119.

41. Lewis, p. 205.

42. *The Old Man and the Sea*, pp. 27-28.

43. Lewis, p. 206.

44. Rovit, p. 89.

45. *The Old Man and the Sea*, p. 13.

46. *The Poems of Emily Dickinson*, II, 647-648.

47. Sheridan Baker, Ernest Hemingway. See Baker's discussion, pp. 126-32.

A SELECTED
BIBLIOGRAPHY

Primary sources

Across the River and Into the Trees. New York: Charles Scribner's Sons, 1950.

Death in the Afternoon. New York: Charles Scribner's Sons, 1932.

A Farewell to Arms. New York: Charles Scribner's Sons, 1929.

For Whom the Bell Tolls. New York: Charles Scribner's Sons, 1940.

Green Hills of Africa. New York: Charles Scribner's Sons, 1935.

Men at War: The Best War Stories of All Times. Edited, with an Introduction by Ernest Hemingway. New York: Crown Publishers, 1942.

The Old Man and the Sea. New York: Charles Scribner's Sons, 1952.

The Short Stories of Ernest Hemingway. New York: Charles Scribner's Sons, 1953.

The Sun Also Rises. New York: Charles Scribner's Sons, 1926.

To Have and Have Not. New York: Charles Scribner's Sons, 1937.

The Torrents of Spring. New York: Charles Scribner's Sons, 1926.

"Two Tales of Darkness: A Man of the World; Get a Seeing-Eyed Dog," *The Atlantic Monthly*, 200:5 (November 1957), 64-68.

secondary sources

Aldridge, John W. *After the Lost Generation*. New York: Noonday Press, 1958.

Anderson, Charles R. "Hemingway's Other Style," *Ernest Hemingway: Critiques of Four Major Novels*. Carlos Baker (ed.). New York: Charles Scribner's Sons, 1962.

Arnold, Lloyd R. *High on the Wild with Hemingway*. Caldwell, Idaho: The Caxton Printers, Ltd., 1968.

A SELECTED BIBLIOGRAPHY

Aronowitz, Alfred G., and Peter Hamill. *Ernest Hemingway: The Life and Death of a Man.* New York: Lancer Books, Inc., 1961.

Atkins, John W. *The Art of Ernest Hemingway: His Work and Personality.* London: Peter Nevill, 1952.

Backman, Melvin. "Hemingway: The Matador and the Crucified," *Hemingway and His Critics.* Carlos Baker (ed.). New York: Hill & Wang, Inc., 1961.

Baker, Carlos. *Ernest Hemingway: A Life Story.* New York: Charles Scribner's Sons, 1969.

————. *Hemingway: The Writer as Artist.* Princeton: Princeton University Press, 1956, 2d ed.

———— (ed.). *Hemingway and His Critics.* New York: Hill & Wang, Inc., 1961.

———— (ed.). *Ernest Hemingway: Critiques of Four Major Novels.* New York: Charles Scribner's Sons, 1962.

Baker, Sheridan. *Ernest Hemingway: An Introduction and Interpretation.* New York: Holt, Rinehart & Winston, Inc., 1967.

Barzun, Jacques. *Classic, Romantic, and Modern.* Garden City, New York: Doubleday & Company, Inc., 1961.

Beach, Joseph Warren. *American Fiction: 1920-1940.* New York: MacMillan Company, 1942.

Beach, Sylvia. *Shakespeare and Company.* New York: Harcourt, Brace & Company, 1959.

Beck, Warren. "The Shorter Happy Life of Mrs. Macomber," *Modern Fiction Studies,* 1 (November 1955), 28-37.

Beebe, Maurice. "Criticism of Ernest Hemingway: A Selected Checklist with an Index to Studies of Separate Works," *Modern Fiction Studies,* 1 (August 1955), 36-45.

Benson, Jackson J. *Hemingway: The Writer's Art of Self-Defense.* Minneapolis: University of Minnesota Press, 1969.

Berne, Eric, M. D. *Games People Play: The Psychology of Human Relationships.* New York: Grove Press, Inc., 1964.

Billington, Ray Allen. *The Far Western Frontier, 1830-1860.* New York: Harper & Row, 1956.

Breit, Harvey. "Talk with Mr. Hemingway," *New York Times Book Review,* September 17, 1950, p. 14.

Brinin, John Malcolm. *The Third Rose: Gertrude Stein and Her World.* Boston: Little, Brown & Company, 1959.

Brooks, Cleanth. *The Hidden God: Studies in Hemingway, Faulkner, Yeats, Eliot, and Warren.* New Haven: Yale University Press, 1963.

Brooks, Van Wyck. *On Literature Today.* New York: E. P. Dutton & Company, 1941.

Burgum, Edwin Berry. *The Novel and the World's Dilemma.* New York: Oxford University Press, 1947.

Burhans, Clinton S., Jr. *"The Old Man and the Sea:* Hemingway's Tragic Vision of Man," *Hemingway and His Critics.* Carlos Baker (ed.). New York: Hill & Wang, Inc., 1961.

Burnam, Tom. "Primitivism and Masculinity in the Work of Ernest Hemingway," *Modern Fiction Studies,* 1 (August 1955), 20-24.

Callaghan, Morley. *That Summer in Paris: Memories of Tangled Friendships with Hemingway, Fitzgerald and Some Others.* New York: Dell Publishing Company, Inc., 1964.

Campbell, Joseph. *The Hero with a Thousand Faces.* New York: Meridian Books, 1960.

————. *The Masks of God: Primitive Mythology.* New York: The Pantheon Press, 1959.

Canby, Henry Seidel. *American Memoir.* Boston: Houghton Mifflin Company, 1947.

Cargill, Oscar. *Intellectual America: Ideas on the March.* New York: The MacMillan Company, 1941.

Clendenning, John. "Hemingway's Gods, Dead and Alive," *Texas Studies in Language and Literature,* III (1962).

Commager, Henry Steele. *The American Mind: An Interpretation of American Thought and Character Since the 1880's.* New Haven: Yale University Press, 1950.

Cowley, Malcolm. *Exile's Return: A Literary Odyssey of the 1920's.* New York: The Viking Press, 1951.

————. "Hemingway and the Hero," *New Republic,* 111 (December 4, 1944), 754-758.

————. Introduction to *The Portable Hemingway.* New York: The Viking Press, Inc., 1944.

De Falco, Joseph M. *The Hero in Hemingway's Short Stories.* Pittsburgh: University of Pittsburgh Press, 1963.

Dickinson, Emily. *The Poems of Emily Dickinson.* 3 vols. Thomas H. Johnson (ed.). Cambridge, Mass.: The Belknap Press of Harvard University Press 1958.

Eastman Max. *Art and the Life of Action.* New York: Alfred A. Knopf, Inc., 1934.

Engstrom, Alfred G. "Dante, Flaubert, and 'The Snows of Kilimanjaro,'" *Modern Language Notes,* 65 (1950), 203-205.

Fenton, Charles A. *The Apprenticeship of Ernest Hemingway: The Early Years.* New York: The Viking Press, Inc., 1958.

Fitzgerald, F. Scott. *The Letters of F. Scott Fitzgerald.* Edited with an Introduction by Andrew Turnbull. New York: Charles Scribner's Sons, 1963.

Frohock, W. M. *The Novel of Violence in America, 1920-1950.* Dallas: Southern Methodist University Press, 1950.

Fromm, Erich. "The Present Human Condition," *The American Scholar,* XXV (Winter 1955-56), 29-35.

Geismar, Maxwell. *The Last of the Provincials: The American Novel, 1915-1925.* Boston: Houghton Mifflin Company, 1947.

————. *Writers in Crisis.* New York: Hill & Wang, Inc., 1961.

Gurko, Leo. *Ernest Hemingway and the Pursuit of Heroism.* New York: Thomas Y. Crowell Company, 1968.

Halliday, E. M. "Hemingway's Ambiguity: Symbolism and Irony," *Hemingway*. Robert P. Weeks (ed.). Englewood Cliffs, New Jersey: Prentice-Hall, Inc., 1962.

————. "Hemingway's Narrative Perspective," *Ernest Hemingway: Critiques of Four Major Novels*. Carlos Baker (ed.). New York: Charles Scribner's Sons, 1962.

Hallowell, Irving A. *The Role of Conjuring in Salteaux Society: Publication of the Philadelphia Anthropological Society,* Vol. II. Philadelphia: University of Pennsylvania Press, 1942.

Handy, William J. "A New Dimension for a Hero: Santiago of *The Old Man and the Sea*," *Six Contemporary Novels*. William O. S. Sutherland, Jr. (ed.). Austin: University of Texas Press, 1962.

Hemingway, Leicester. *My Brother, Ernest Hemingway*. Cleveland: World Publishing Company, 1962.

Hemingway, Mary. "The Making of a Book: A Chronicle and a Memoir," *New York Times Book Review,* May 10, 1964, pp. 26-27.

Hicks, Granville. *The Great Tradition: An Interpretation of American Literature Since the Civil War,* revised. New York: International Publishers, 1935.

Hoffman, Frederick and Olga Vickery. *William Faulkner: Two Decades of Criticism*. East Lansing: Michigan State College Press, 1951.

Hotchner, A. E. *Papa Hemingway*. New York: Random House, Inc., 1966.

Inge, William Ralph. *Christian Mysticism*. New York: Charles Scribner's Sons, 1899.

James, William. *Essays in Pragmatism*. Edited with an Introduction by Alburey Castell. New York: Hafner Publishing Company, 1961.

Jung, C. G. *Psychology of the Unconscious: A Study of the Transformations and Symbolisms of the Libido*. Translated with an Introduction by Beatrice M. Hinkle, M.D. New York: Dodd, Mead and Company, 1947.

————. *Two Essays on Analytical Psychology.* Translated by R. F. C. Hull. Cleveland: World Publishing Company, 1961.

Kazin, Alfred. *On Native Grounds: An Interpretation of Modern American Prose Literautre.* Garden City, New York: Doubleday & Company, Inc., 1956.

Killinger, John. *Hemingway and the Dead Gods: A Study in Existentialism.* Lexington: University of Kentucky Press, 1960.

Lewis, Robert W., Jr. *Hemingway on Love.* Austin: University of Texas Press, 1965.

Light, James F. "The Religion of Death in *A Farewell to Arms,*" *Ernest Hemingway: Critiques of Four Major Novels.* Carlos Baker (ed.). New York: Charles Scribner's Sons, 1962.

McCaffery, John K. M. (ed.). *Ernest Hemingway: The Man and His Work.* Cleveland: World Publishing Company, 1950.

Mizener, Arthur. "The Two Hemingways," *The Great Experiment in American Literature.* Carl Bode (ed.) London: William Heinemann, 1961.

————. *The Far Side of Paradise: A Biography of F. Scott Fitzgerald.* Boston: Houghton Mifflin Company, 1951.

Montgomery, Constance Cappel. *Hemingway in Michigan.* New York: Fleet Publishing Company, 1966.

Moynihan, William R. "The Martyrdom of Robert Jordan," *College English,* 21 (December 1959), 127-132.

Perkins, Maxwell. *Editor to Author: The Letters of Maxwell E. Perkins.* Edited with an Introduction by John Hall Wheelock. New York: Charles Scribner's Sons, 1950.

Paolini, Pier Francesco. "The Hemingway of the Major Works," *Hemingway and His Critics.* Carlos Baker (ed.). New York: Hill & Wang, Inc., 1961.

Plimpton, George. "Ernest Hemingway," *Writers at Work: The "Paris Review" Interviews.* Second series. New York: Viking Press, Inc., 1963.

Riesman, David, *et al. The Lonely Crowd: A Study of the Changing American Character*. New York: Doubleday & Company, Inc., 1955.

Rovit, Earl. *Ernest Hemingway*. New York: Twayne Publishers, Inc., 1963.

Salinger, J. D. *The Catcher in the Rye*. Boston: Little, Brown & Company, 1951.

Samuels, Lee. *A Hemingway Check List*. New York: Charles Scribner's Sons, 1951.

Sanderson, Stewart F. *Ernest Hemingway*. New York: Grove Press, 1961.

Sanford, Marcelline Hemingway. *At the Hemingways: A Family Portrait*. Boston: Atlantic-Little, Brown, 1962.

Scott, Arthur L. "In Defense of Robert Cohn," *College English,* 18 (March 1957), 309-314.

Shroder, Maurice Z. "The Novel as a Genre," *The Theory of the Novel*. Philip Stevick (ed.). New York: The Free Press, 1967.

Snell, George. *The Shapers of American Fiction, 1798-1947*. New York: E. P. Dutton & Company, Inc., 1947.

Soloviev. *A Solovyov Anthology*. S. L. Frank (ed.). Translated by Natalie Dunnington. New York: Charles Scribner's Sons, 1950.

Somerset, Fitzroy Richard, 4th Baron of Raglan. *The Hero: A Study in Tradition, Myth, and Drama*. New York: Vintage Books, 1956.

Spilka, Mark. "The Death of Love in *The Sun Also Rises,*" *Ernest Hemingway: Critiques of Four Major Novels*. Carlos Baker (ed.). New York: Charles Scribner's Sons, 1962.

Stein, William Bysshe. "Love and Lust in Hemingway's Short Stories," *Texas Studies in Literature and Language,* 3 (Summer 1961), 234-242.

Stephens, Robert O. "Hemingway's Don Quixote in Pamplona," *College English* 23 (December 1961), 216-218.

Thoreau, Henry David. *Walden.* Edited with an Introduction and Notes by Sherman Paul. Boston: Houghton Mifflin Company, 1957.

Trilling, Lionel. "Hemingway and His Critics,' *Hemingway and His Critics.* Carlos Baker (ed.). New York: Hill & Wang, Inc., 1961.

Van Doren, Carl. *The American Novel, 1789-1939.* New York: The MacMillan Company, 1940.

Warren, Robert Penn. "Introduction," *A Farewell to Arms.* New York: Charles Scribner's Sons, 1953.

Weeks, Robert P. "Fakery in *The Old Man and the Sea*," *College English,* 24 (December 1962), 188-192.

———— (ed.). *Hemingway: A Collection of Critical Essays.* Englewood Cliffs, N.J.: Prentice-Hall, Inc., 1962.

West, Ray B., Jr. "Ernest Hemingway: The Failure of Sensibility," *Forms of Modern Fiction: Essays Collected in Honor of Joseph Warren Beach.* William Van O'Connor (ed.) Minneapolis: The University of Minnesota Press, 1948.

Westbrook, Max. "The Archetypal Ethic of *The Ox-Bow Incident*," *Western American Literature,* I (Summer 1966), 105-118.

————. "The Stewardship of Ernest Hemingway," *The Texas Quarterly* (Winter 1966), 89-101.

Wilson, Edmund. *The Shores of Light.* New York: Farrar, Straus & Young, Inc., 1952.

————. *The Wound and the Bow: Seven Studies in Literature.* Boston: Houghton Mifflin Company, 1941.

Young, Philip. *Ernest Hemingway.* New York: Rinehart & Company, Inc., 1952.

————. "Our Hemingway Man," *The Kenyon Review,* 26 (Autumn 1964), 676-707.

INDEX

SINCE EACH CHAPTER deals individually with a single novel, no attempt is made to list page references to particular characters from the novel treated in the chapter. References to characters from a novel not being considered directly in the chapter are indexed, however.

253